Jesus Christ said,
"My Words are Spirit and they are LIFE."

# BIBLE ANSWERS FOR JEHOVAH'S WITNESSES

# for Jehovah's Witnesses

by Charles Trombley

Author: **Kicked Out of the Kingdom; Visitation, the Key to Church Growth,** and **Have Spiritual Gifts Ceased?**

*Bible Answers for Jehovah's Witnesses*
by Charles Trombley


Expositor Publications
293 West Ithica
Broken Arrow, Oklahoma 74012

Printed in the United States of America
Faith Printing Company
Taylors, South Carolina 29687

## INTRODUCTION

Religion is on the increase with the Jehovah's Witnesses leading the race. Their increases the last few years outstrip all other religious groups anywhere. At present they have more ordained ministers than both the Protestant and Catholic bodies combined. Of course, every Witness is a minister, but what other group can boast that every *one* of their members is actively crusading for their cause?

When I use the term religionist or cultist, I'm not being unkind or ridiculing. They're inclusive terms, embracing any religious theology that rejects the historical and Biblical position of Jesus Christ as both Lord and God manifested in the flesh having laid aside His eternal glory, made in the form of subjected man, providing complete and final redemption from all the works of sin through His sacrificial death, burial and bodily resurrection.

Most cultists are hungry souls, tired of the unsatisfying formalism, comfortable pews, and lukewarm pulpits. Theirs is a desire for Biblical literalness and reality as they search for man's existence and future. They use the name Christian because in all honesty they believe themselves to be so. Let's examine that claim and see.

## TABLE OF CONTENTS

**Section III Bible Answers for Watchtower Questions**

# I

# THE HISTORY OF THE WATCH TOWER

## CHAPTER 1 – WHO ARE THE JEHOVAH'S WITNESSES?

"Honestly examining the facts about them, and comparing the facts with the Holy Scriptures of the Bible, we are led irresistibly to the conclusion that Jehovah's Witnesses are the Bible Christians of today. *They are the only ones preaching the good news of God's established Kingdom" (Christendom or Christianity,* pp. 16, 17).

Is this true? Are these hyperactive people, systematically preaching from door to door warning men to "flee to the safety of the Watch Tower Society lest they be destroyed in Armageddon," really the Bible Christians of today?

If you'll listen attentively you'll discover they have no personal assurance of salvation from sin or knowledge of the Living Christ. In fact the "facts" reveal they don't even *want* to receive Bible salvation, but they're feverously working to prove themselves worthy of escaping God's great wrath at Armageddon. And if they do succeed they still aren't sure of salvation; they've only gained the opportunity to live another 1,000 years of probation on earth. Only after successfully passing a final test can they gain everlasting life on earth.

They are correct in saying they're the *only* ones preaching the gospel of the established kingdom, meaning the secret return of Jesus in 1914 to head the Watch Tower Organization.

Their name, Jehovah's Witnesses, is recent, adopted by the late Judge Rutherford, the Society's second president, in 1931. It wasn't until 1938 that they became Jehovah's New World Society, and as such not subject to any man on earth. All government, all religion, and all commerce is of the devil.

Under the direction of the President-General Manager, who is the Vicar and Vicegerent of Christ's established kingdom, new light is dispensed through the Channel of Communication, *The Watchtower* magazine. Because the Society declares itself to be that "Faithful and Wise Servant Class" (See Matt. 24:25-27), it reserves the right to interpret all scripture for its disciples. Actually, this top-down control has evolved to the place where every talk given in the Kingdom Hall, every sermonette preached at the front door, and all books studied are directly controlled through prepared literature. Two men, the General Manager and the Director of the Publicity Department, have the final say on everything printed resulting in all Witnesses saying and doing the same thing at the same time.

## ARE THEY THE ONLY ONES WITH THIS MESSAGE?

If you mean the message of God's established kingdom, yes. Only the Society believes Jesus returned secretly in 1914-1918 and established His Kingdom. He now rules amidst His enemies, using the Society as His physical administrator. However, they are not the only ones holding their particular doctrines. They're actually the largest and most active disciples orbiting around the teachings of Charles Russell, the movement's founder.

There may be others but I personally know of at least ten such groups: the Freytag Movement, the Pastoral Bible Institute, the Standard Bible Students, the Associated Bible Students, the Laymen's Home Missionary Movement, the Servants of Yah, the Back to the Bible Way, the Free Earnest Bible Students, the Bible Students of England, and the International Bible Students, known also as the Dawn Bible Students.

Not all of these groups accept the "established kingdom" theory but their foundations are laid in Russell's theology. Of these, the Dawn Bible Students are the largest and the only group with a national headquarters of any size and a well-equipped publishing house in Rutherford, New Jersey. Their former radio program, "The Frank and Ernest Broadcast" was heard on more than 300 stations.

## THEY MUST REALLY BE ZEALOUS FOR GOD. LOOK AT HOW MANY OF THEM GO DOOR TO DOOR!

No one denies their interest in religious matters, but like the Jews in Paul's day, they seek to establish their own righteousness – having rejected God's righteousness through faith in Jesus Christ. Don't misunderstand their intense activity! It isn't based on a love for the souls of man but is their way of earning their salvation.

True Witnessing is an expression of "that which we have seen and heard" (1 John 1:3). Namely that our sins are forgiven and we are enjoying fellowship with God through Jesus Christ our Lord. Jehovah's Witnesses, however, view their door-to-door "preaching" as worship, a means of proving themselves "worthy" of surviving Armageddon's destruction. They're motivated by fear. They have no message of completed salvation or freedom from sin. In fact they don't believe you *can* be born again, spirit filled, or have unbroken fellowship with God as His child. Only 144,000 can achieve that!

Yet they continue to grow. In 1973, 1,758,429 publishers logged nearly 292 million hours of door-to-door preaching. It isn't a striking growth but relatively steady. In 1972 it took ten Witnesses nearly 1800 hours of recorded service to gain one convert to baptism, representing an increase of 3.8 percent according to the 1973 *Yearbook.*

At the same time hundreds of thousands are leaving the movement. *The Watchtower* (9/1/69) had an article, "Where Are The 200,000?" During the 20-year period between 1949 and 1968, some 200,000 had quit preaching. Bringing the statistics up to date (1974) more than 400,000 have fallen out of the "ark."

This book is to help them. ARE JEHOVAH'S WITNESSES CHRISTIAN? Let's take a look at what they believe before we judge!

## CHAPTER 2 – WHO STARTED THE MOVEMENT?

"Although God has had his witnesses on earth for almost sixty centuries, only in modern times did they draw together for organized worldwide work."

In substantiating this claim they point to the Apostles John and Paul, Arius, Waldo, Wycliff, and Martin Luther as connecting links. Arius (c. 256-336), however, is the only one that modern Watchtowerism can identify with. He was a Libyan Catholic theologican in Alexandria who denied the full deity of Jesus and was condemned in the Council of Nicea (325 A.D.). If the other "Messengers" were alive today they would publicly disclaim and rebuke them for their error. Their writings leave the Watch Tower claim wanting.

Like many founders of religions, Russell's early followers heralded him as the "greatest reformer since the Apostle Paul."

"It became necessary for Jehovah, in fulfillment of his own prophecy, to raise up his witnesses in these modern times, *not as a new religion,* but as a climax to the long succession of Witnesses" *(Jehovah's Witnesses in the Divine Purpose,* p. 10).

But all he actually did was take Arius' denial of Jesus' deity, and following through with the Socinian heresy and early Adventism, finally arrived with "another gospel," "another Jesus," and "another means of salvation." IT WAS A NEW RELIGION!

### THE APOSTLE OF REASON

Charles Russell was born in Pittsburg (Old Allegheny), Pennsylvania in 1852. In his own words we read:

"We begin the narrative at the year 1868 (when he was sixteen), the editor of *Zion's Watch Tower,* having been a consecrated child of God for some years, and a member of the Congregational Church and the Y.M.C.A., began to be shaken in faith regarding many long accepted doctrines.

"Brought up a Presbyterian, indoctrinated from the Catechism, and being naturally of an inquiring mind, I fell prey to the *logic of infidelity,* AS SOON AS I BEGAN TO THINK FOR MYSELF."

While trying to convince an infidel friend of Christianity he found the doctrine of eternal torment revolting, resulting in his rejecting the Bible as long as it remained in it. Then he studied several oriental religions, but still wasn't able to find satisfaction. For the next two years, between the ages of 16 and 18, he continued in his floundering agnosticism, reason, and logical unbelief, pondering Christianity, unable to accept it, and yet not willing to let it go.

In 1870 he wrote:

"Seemingly by accident, one evening I dropped into a dusty, dingy hall in Allegheny, Pennsylvania, where I had heard religious services were held. . . . There, for the first time, I heard something of the views of Second Adventism, by Jonas Wendell . . . " *(Jehovah's Witnesses in the Divine Plan,* p. 14).

As a result, his interest in the Bible was rekindled and he returned to a study "with more zeal and care then ever before." He continues:

"I soon began to see that we were living somewhere near the close of the Gospel Age, and near the time when the Lord declared that the wise, watching ones of His children should come to a clear knowledge of His plan."

This wasn't a new concept. Miller, in 1816, predicted Christ's return in 1843 or 1844, while Bengel set the date for 1836. In England, the Irvingites set several dates between 1835 and 1866. While most of them looked for a visible Advent, some taught differently. Among these was H.B. Rice, who looked for an invisible return in 1870 as did a group of disappointed Second Adventists headed by N.H. Barbour of Rochester, New York, who set the date for 1874 or 1875.

These Adventists (Millerites) had "hoped" for a visible advent in 1844 but they hoped in vain. Russell was grieved at their error and wrote: "These wrong views so generally held of both the object and manner of Christ's Second Advent led me to write a pamphlet: *The Object and Manner of the Lord's Return."* The Lord's return would be invisible, he said, apparently influenced by his alliance with Barbour.

And so the boy Russell, at the tender age of 18, with renewed vigor to "reason the Scriptures," formed a Bible study group. It was this group that titled him "Pastor" in 1876. "The period from 1870 to 1875 was a time of constant growth," he said.

"However, we were then merely getting the outlines for God's plan and *unlearning many cherished errors,* the time for the clear discernment of the minutia not having fully come."

Notice what precipitated this!

As a Congregational boy he often chalked Bible texts on public walls warning people to flee the torments of hell. This inward fear apparently plagued him, frightening him into rejecting God's word as written. So the Bible hell became the first "cherished error" he unlearned. Had he submitted his life to Christ, repented of his infidelity and logic of reason, and trusted Christ as his Saviour, the fear of hell would have vanished with the knowledge that his sins were already forgiven!

Once the step was taken he passionately attacked God's judgments. After one violent tirade a liberal clergyman in Pittsburg remarked, "I'm glad to see you turn the hose on hell and put the fire out."

"IF the Bible does teach that eternal torture is the fate of all except the saints, it should be preached, yes thundered from the housetops, weekly, daily, hourly; if it does not so teach, the fact should be made known, and the foul stain dishonoring God's holy name be removed," he replied.

Guided by the "logic of infidelity" and his fear of hell, he gradually abandoned every major Bible truth he once held. He did accept the Bible again but only after he satisfactorily changed many "truths" to conform to his logic. His method of using Scripture to prove a previously conceived theory remained in evidence throughout his life. Any Christian can testify that even though the Bible is learned as fact, it must be quickened by the Spirit before it becomes reality. His method required no faith or spiritual illumination but simply, "Come let us reason together." He rejected the Trinity as unreasonable, hell as illogical, and the personality of the Spirit as impossible. THERE ISN'T ANY EVIDENCE HE EVER GRADUATED OR WAS DELIVERED FROM THE LOGIC OF INFIDELITY! Apparently he became interested in a novel approach to Bible study.

He finally joined the Adventists in 1876. Then, while busy with his study group, he met N.H. Barbour who taught that Jesus had already returned invisibly in 1874. He was thrilled to discover another person who agreed with his views although the evidence indicates he was already familiar with Barbour's dates. Someone in Barbour's group introduced him to *The Emphatic Diaglott*, a corrupt Greek interlinear by Benjamin Wilson, a Christadelphian and Unitarian.

Standing alone against every other reputable translation, Wilson erroneously translated the Greek word *parousia* in Matthew 24:3 as "presence." This single word, along with a maze of chronological guesswork, led Barbour to conclude Christ's Advent would be invisible. Russell accepted the apparent evidence (he never studied or knew Greek) and began teaching Barbour's revelation date of 1874 as the time of Christ's invisible presence.

Because of their mutual interest Russell combined his Pittsburg study group with Barbour's Rochester group. Working together they co-published the book *Three Worlds* in which they chronologically dated that "The Times of the Gentiles" would end in 1914. So as early as 1877 Russell was on written record as saying that Christ had secretly returned in 1874. He then curtailed his inherited clothing stores, selling them for a quarter million dollars, and launched into a preaching career that lasted 42 years and influenced millions of lives.

## CHAPTER 3 – HOW DID HE INFLUENCE SO MANY PEOPLE?

From the beginning Russell realized that most people don't think; they simply follow. So he combined this trait with current events – a practice the Witnesses still follow – and amazed multitudes with his prophetic statements.

In 1889 he predicted in *The Time Is at Hand* that the Kingdom of God would crush the Gentile Image in 1915 and the *last* member of the Body of Christ would be glorified some time *before the end of 1914,* and the great tribulation would end *then.* It electrified those who heard him and it didn't take him long to persuade them to abandon their "cherished errors." Awestruck people said, "Never has one spoken so forcefully and authoritatively as that 'faithful and wise servant' who rediscovered the true teachings of Jesus as taught by the Apostles."

Russell and Barbour split in 1878 as co-editors of *The Herald of the Morning* magazine over Barbour's article on the atonement. Just what the difference was I can't find out, but Russell's own views on the atonement were far from scriptural. A year later, in 1879, our youthful "Apostle of Reason" founded *Zion's Watchtower,* the forerunner of the present *The Watchtower Announcing Jehovah's Kingdom.* Little did he realize that the first run of 6,000 copies would one day exceed 12 million copies monthly.

Reworking doctrines proved to be no problem for Charles. Arbitrarily lifting passages out of context (the best method for debunking their conclusions is by reading the passage in its proper context), he systematically invented "another gospel," with "another Jesus," and motivated by "another spirit."

It's difficult to understand how a person with "a naturally inquiring mind" could so easily reject truth, but he did! True, it requires faith to accept "cherished errors" of the church when you view the coldness, careless living, etc., but it takes much more faith to accept and publicly preach the far-fetched theories, unfulfilled prophecies, and doctrines with nothing more to stand on than the promises, new translations, and chronological speculations of one who claims to be of the "faithful and wise servant class."

Having carefully laid the foundation for his "gospel of reason," he and six other men applied for and received a charter for Zion's Watch Tower Tract Society in Allegheny County, Pennsylvania, in 1884. Thus was born the modern Watch Tower Society.

Two years later he published the first volume of the *Millennium Dawn* series, *The Divine Plan of the Ages.* These six books, now known as *Studies in the Scriptures,* are the foundational textbooks around which the satellite groups revolve.

He assumed he was that "Faithful and Wise Servant" of Matthew 24:25-27, and the ruler of the Lord's household. He eventually became so convinced he wrote:

"If anyone lays the *Scripture Studies* aside, even after he has used them – if he lays them aside and ignores them and goes to the Bible alone, though he has understood the Bible for ten years – if he lays them aside, he goes into darkness. On the other hand, if he had merely read the *Scripture Studies* with their references and had not read a page of the Bible as such, he would be in the light at the end of two years" *(The Watchtower,* 9/15/10, p. 298).

That principle still exists! No one ever became a Jehovah's Witness just by studying the Bible; *they must have a Watch Tower book as a study guide.* At best their studies are "book studies" where the Bible is used as a commentary on the book.

Could it be that he was fearful that if one read the Word under the guidance of the Holy Spirit as the Bible declares (1

John 2:27), they might loose his "truths" and discover the real truth?

## CHAPTER 4 – WHY ARE THEY CALLED A CULT?

Recognizing them as a cult and hating them are two different things. Christians don't – or shouldn't – hate them or any other person. But as part of their indoctrination the Witnesses are taught that rejection or even questioning their doctrines is tantamount to hatred. They are classified as cultists because of their outright denial of the Deity of Jesus Christ and His bodily resurrection.

When Russell substituted logic for faith he opened himself wide for all kinds of demonic deceptions. Denying the Deity of Jesus was easy. Piecing together the ancient heresy of Arius, he declared Jesus was no longer the *only* begotten, but only the first created. All angels, including Lucifer who became the devil, were his fellow-created brothers. He held the unique position as "a god" because he was the first created. Rather than restoring Apostolic understanding, he brought forth two gods.

Jehovah, the Almighty, created the lesser god, Jesus, as the first and only direct act of creation. Therefore, there are two gods, a big one and a little one, the Almighty and the mighty. And wonders of wonders, through all this semantic double-talk, they insist they're not polytheistic.

## CHAPTER 5 – DID HIS PREDICTIONS COME TO PASS?

He never really knew. He died aboard a transcontinental train in Pampa, Texas, in 1916, but enough time had passed to cause him untold heartache.

"Suppose 1915 should pass with the world's affairs all serene and with evidence that the 'very elect' had not been changed and without the restoration of natural Israel to favor under the New Covenant. What then? And would not that prove a keen disappointment? Indeed it would! It would work IRREPARABLE WRECK to the parallel dispensations, and Israel's double, and to the Jubilee Calculations, and to the prophecy of the 2300 days of Daniel, and to the epoch called the 'Gentile Times' and to the 1260, 1290, and 1335 days. . . . None of these would be available any longer. . . ."

When he wrote *The Time Is at Hand* he predicted that the *last* member of the 144,000 (the Body of Christ) would be glorified and raptured sometime BEFORE THE END OF 1914. He lived until 1916, proving either his calculations were wrong or he wasn't one of the faithful 144,000. Strange also that a few years later, Rutherford, his successor, would begin filling in that number so that today there are still a few thousand of them walking the earth.

Ironically, both the physical and spiritual aspects of his predictions failed! He said the Great Tribulation would *end* in 1914. Modern Watchtower witnesses are now waiting for it to climax at Armageddon in 1975. And rather than God crushing the Gentile image and bringing about world peace with the start of the Millennium, World War I came and since that time even greater wars and rumors of wars. Israel has yet to be restored to favor under the New Covenant (Rom. 11:25).

One's Christian compassion goes out to a man like Russell and his deluded disciples. Every one of his predictions, like those of so many men before and after him, failed! And like many others, he created explanations to cover the errors. The 50-year period between 1874 and 1914 didn't prove to be the "Day of God's Wrath," neither did Jehovah separate the wheat from the tares. Instead, modern Witnesses of the Watch Tower, his spiritual offspring, claim to be doing that separation through their door-to-door activities.

## CHAPTER 6 – WAS HE A FALSE PROPHET THEN?

"When a prophet (or any man) speaks in the name of the Lord, if the thing follow not, nor come to pass, that is the thing which the Lord hath not spoken" (Deut. 18:22).

Either he was a thoroughly deceived, self-appointed prophet – or a deliberate sensationalist – or totally insane.

Obviously after his death, the Watch Tower Society was obligated to explain away his false prophecies – or go out of business. Cultism dies hard and Watchtowerism is no exception. Like every cult leader before him, Rutherford, Russell's successor, cleverly sidestepped the issue. Later he actually muddied the already murky waters by changing the date of the invisible Advent from 1874 to 1914 and claimed "added light," which gave him a more perfect understanding of what Russell really meant. Whenever the Society declares a major doctrinal change – and they have had several – their stock answer is "added light," and everyone in the movement accepts it as a satisfactory answer.

If Russell was correct, as thousands of his disciples believe, and Jesus returned secretly in 1874, then Rutherford and his disciples are in error – but, if Rutherford's "added light" is right, then the satellite believers and Russell were deceived. Meanwhile, both camps hurl charges of "evil servants" at the other.

During his lifetime Russell proved to be a highly colorful character, with his last 12 years blotted with trials and apparent scandals. In 1879, after 18 years of marriage, Mrs. Russell left her husband and in 1903 sued for separation. Although she never believed her husband was guilty of actual adultery, she did give sworn testimony that his conduct with one Rose Ball was far from proper.

At the time he declared he was without funds, but he settled in 1909 by paying his wife $6,036.00. (During litigation which lasted three years, it was disclosed that several societies existed through which the Pastor carried on his religious work. All income derived from these societies was under the control of a holding company, in which Russell held $990.00 of the $1,000.00 capital and two of his followers the other $10.00. Obviously he controlled the entire financial power of the Society and was unaccountable to anyone.)

His difficulties did not end with his marital problem. In 1913 the *Brooklyn Daily Eagle* published a cartoon picturing the Pastor and his "Miracle Wheat" in such a way that Russell sued for $100,000.00 damages. It seems *The Watch Tower* publication advertised wheat seed for sale at $1.00 a pound, asserting it would grow five times as much as any other brand of wheat. The profits, of course, would be used to publish the Pastor's sermons. When the Government stepped in and investigated, the wheat was found to be low in tests and non-miraculous in all ways. Consequently the *Eagle* won the case. No one wants to judge unfairly but obviously the wheat was a religious gimmick to raise funds. Modern Witnesses, however, insist it was only the invention of "jealous religionists" who were trying to reproach the good Pastor's name. The above material can be documented so it's hardly an invention.

If that wasn't enough, on March 17 of the same year, he sued the Reverend J.H. Ross, Pastor of the James Street Baptist Church, Hamilton, Ontario, for libel. In June 1912, Ross had published a pamphlet entitled *Some Facts About the Self-Styled Pastor Charles T. Russell* which frankly denounced him as an unqualified minister. He minced no words in rebuking the whole system as "anti-rational, anti-scientific, anti-Biblical, anti-Christian, and a deplorable perversion of the gospel of God's dear Son."

Russell had no choice but to sue. This type of suit forced him to prove the charges against him were false. He admitted under oath, during some five hours of cross-examination, that his education ended with the seventh grade. Having just told the court that he knew both Greek and Hebrew, he was forced to admit, under embarrassing circumstances, that he didn't even know the letters of the Greek alphabet.

Trapped with no way out, he was forced by Ross's attorney to admit that he had never been ordained, had never furthered his education, knew neither Greek, Hebrew or Latin; he swore his wife had *not* divorced him, nor had the court granted her alimony. Rather than winning his case against Ross, he publicly branded himself a perjurer. The court's verdict was "No Bill."

Nothing more can be gained by further exposing this man's character. He denied every cardinal doctrine of the Bible, basing many of his rejections on a more perfect understanding of the Greek language, of which he knew nothing. This doesn't mean that God can't or doesn't use unlettered servants – He does and will continue to do so – but Russell made claims that just weren't true!

This is strange for the man who wrote in *The Watch Tower* (9/15/09) that he was "that servant Jesus referred to in Matthew 24:25-27." Strange indeed, that this man who said he was the "seventh messenger" to the church age should have to misrepresent the facts of his true life – this man who said that anyone studying his *Studies in the Scriptures* could find the truth and understand God's Plan without even reading the Bible. Strange indeed, yet the Organization he began survives today.

A false prophet? Yes! This doubting youth, this Apostle of Reason, this great reformer and revealer of lost truth and the true plan of salvation, built his movement upon the hollow labyrinth of natural reason and, like Adam, "ate of the tree of knowledge of good and evil," while missing the "tree of life."

## CHAPTER 7 – WHAT KIND OF MAN SUCCEEDED HIM?

If Russell was an "Apostle of Reason" then Judge Rutherford was a "Prophet of Hate." Born in 1869 on a Missouri farm, he worked his way through law school. At 22, he was admitted to the Missouri bar and practiced law at Booneville, later serving two years as public prosecutor. He was then appointed as special judge in the 14th District of Missouri.

He said he was contacted by Watchtower pioneers in 1894 and became genuinely interested in Russell's books. His study and involvement brought him an appointment in 1907 as the legal counsellor at the Pittsburg headquarters. When the organization moved to their new Brooklyn offices in 1909 he moved with them and remained there until assuming Russell's position in 1917.

Temperamentally, the men were opposites. While Russell thrived on being a popular idol, Rutherford shunned public appearances. The former was diplomatic, warm and possessed a definite charism; the Judge was cold, hostile and reserved. Russell appealed to the public with his wit and satire by attacking doctrines; the Judge plowed into the cold churches, building quite a reputation for ridiculing individuals.

Shortly after becoming President he found a loophole in the charter and through subterfuge and legal trickeries dissolved the Board of Directors who, according to Russell's will, were to have charge of the work. The ruckus that followed resulted in purging the Society of all Russellites. Those leaving formed the Dawn Bible Students Association and the Laymen's Home Missionary Movement. Had these Board members remained it is doubtful that the modern Society would exist as it does today. Undoubtedly they would have adhered closely to Russell's theology, but Rutherford demanded strict confirmity to his doctrine and organization.

## TROUBLED WATERS PITCH THE ARK

At Bethel dining room that summer on July 17, 1917, he exploded his first of several bombs when he released *The Finished Mystery,* supposedly Russell's seventh volume of *The Millennial Dawn* series. Critics believe that Russell's only claims to this posthumous book were some quotations from his pen. The denunciation of patriotism that sifted through the book was not typical of Russell's beliefs, but of Rutherford's personal hatreds, as his later life proved.

Using fear as a hammer, the Judge and his associates forced the acceptance of this book. Rejection brought threats of excommunication and classification as the "Judas Class" with destruction in the second death. The use of fear, still practiced today, originated with Rutherford and is used by the Society as a means of holding its disciples in line. How different from Jesus who said, "If you love me keep my commandments," not out of fear but because you love and trust me.

As a result of this book, the Judge and seven of his coworkers were jailed in 1918 in the Federal Prison in Atlanta for what the government called un-American activities. The Society's explanation was someone's use of a wireless radio during the war. Later, in order to justify such a state of affairs, they tried to make it appear that their persecutions fulfilled the 42 months of Revelation 11:2 *(Jehovah's Witnesses in the Divine Purpose,* p. 79).

As expected from one who doesn't know Christ personally, Rutherford's solitude in prison did little to temper his bitter disposition. Immediately upon his release his pen spued forth a sour stream of venom and wrath, specifically blaming the clergy for World War I and his imprisonment. It was during this time that public disapproval reached its apex, primarily because of his repetitive rantings and hostile, overbearing attitude toward all other religions.

Troubled without by noxious public relations and within from Russell's conclusively false prophecies, the "Ark of Refuge" from Armageddon's storms was pitching wildly, but his melancholic nature proved he could weather the storm.

Scratching through the ruins of Russell's IRREPARABLE WRECK, he had a brand new set of theories ready within two years, which would become Watchtower theology. "The Kingdom really came as predicted," he said, "but not on earth; it was established in the heavenlies." This established kingdom is *the* gospel of the Watch Tower Witnesses today.

From his angry lips came the "added light" that Christ had suddenly come to His temple in 1918 (cancelling Russell's 1874 theory) for the judgment of Christendom and the Russellites, joined there by the "heavenly class" of 144,000 true witnesses. Included in his revelation was a resurrection that supposedly occurred in 1918.

Theoretically the judgment went against Christendom and she became "Babylon the Great." The remnant who persisted in following Russell was branded as "The Evil Servant Class." Among the nations, the "sheep nations" were those accepting His Established Government of the Watchtower Kingdom, while the "goat nations" were those who rejected or dared to question his claims.

Rather than abandoning Russell's IRREPARABLE WRECK of unfulfilled chronology, he built squarely upon it, KNOWING IT TO BE A FAILURE! Between 1914 and some future Armageddon, he said, there would emerge a "Great Multitude" who would inherit the Watchtower Kingdom on earth, that is, if they successfully survive Armageddon.

Remember that Russell established himself as "that faithful and wise servant, whom his lord hath made ruler of his household, to give them meat in due season" (Matt. 24:45). The Watch Tower publications became the Channels of Communications through which the Divine Will was revealed. Eventually his disciples referred to him as Jehovah's mouthpiece.

Rutherford merely changed the same error and declared the Watch Tower Society was that servant *class.* That spiritual dictatorship is still so deeply ingrained that modern Witnesses boast of talking alike, thinking alike, acting alike, and that this worldwide "unity" is a sign of Jehovah's approval. It's called Theocratic mindedness. It actually suggests a masterful job of preconditioned thinking.

Clearly then, the Kingdom of Jehovah's Witnesses is a substitute, founded on Russell's logical infidelity, natural reason and his IRREPARABLE WRECK OF BIBLE CHRONOLOGY.

## CHAPTER 8 – WAS RUTHERFORD A FALSE PROPHET ALSO?

On September 25, 1920, he gave a public lecture called "Millions Now Living Shall Never Die After 1925." He rented huge billboard advertisements which screamed: MILLIONS NOW LIVING SHALL NEVER DIE!

Using Russell's IRREPARABLE WRECK OF THE JUBILEE CYCLES, he tried to prove the antitypical Jubilee would come in 1925. At that time, he said, all the "ancient worthies" from Abel to John the Baptist would be bodily resurrected, and from 1925 onward, all Adamic death would end and no more "crepes would be hanging on the doors." In other words, no more death after 1925! "Scriptures definitely fix the fact that there will be a resurrection . . . we may expect 1925 to witness the return of these faithful men of Israel . . . " *(Millions Now Living,* p. 88).

Startling? He intended it to be! Those who didn't want to die (and who does?) were quickly attracted to his promissory promotionalism. Russell was a date setter but honest enough to state that IF he was wrong his whole system of chronology was wrong. But Rutherford, leaning on his progressive revelation theory, claimed "added light."

When 1925 came and people continued to die – and the "ancient worthies" failed to appear – he casually covered his tracks by switching the emphasis to "advertising the King and the Kingdom." Because no Witness dares question Jehovah's mouthpiece, *mistakes* are easily whitewashed with "added light."

Three years later in 1928 he encouraged them to continue to look, but the date because of "new revelation"(?) was a "comparatively short time." The next year he bolstered their sagging hopes and proved his fanaticism by building a palatial mansion in San Diego for the "ancient worthies" to live in when they arrived. Naming it Beth Sharim, the "house of princes," the Judge even purchased a high-priced auto for them to drive, although he used it himself. The property was sold after his death in 1942, but only after city officials refused to allow it to be used as a shrine for the Judge.

When objectively studying his administration, one fact appears. The primary aim of the Society was to increase the sale of literature. Therefore it was easy to drown his false prophecies with the stirring cry to "advertise."

## A NEW AGE EMERGES

If Russell gradually reasoned away his "cherished errors," Rutherford quickly swept them away with his pen. The "garment of salvation" (Isa. 61:10) was changed from Christ's covering for the believer's sin to mean God's approval since 1918 of those cooperating with the Society's program. No longer was spiritual growth necessary (this is impossible since no one can be born again or spirit filled except the 144,000), but the latecomers need not despair. One could become a Christian now by "taking in knowledge" by studying Watch Tower books written by the Judge and selling those books as "advertising." This advertising was established as a new kind of worship.

A shift was made from Russell's emphasis on the atonement and the restitution of all things to vindication of Jehovah's name. Perhaps this is why their message centers on the Jehovah of the Old Testament rather than the Jesus of the New. Spirituality was determined by quotas for preaching, book placing, attendance, back calls, etc., and faithfully reported to the Society. Russell's emphasis on personal Bible study was replaced with servicing the neighborhood within their assigned districts. To encourage zeal among the brothers, he offered two free books for every one they sold. (All Jehovah's Witnesses must purchase their own literature for resale.) Thus they served Jehovah directly regardless of public opinion. Vindication of Jehovah's name was foremost and salvation only secondary. It remains so today.

Rutherford declared that God had a certain time to reveal truths; he was that chosen vessel and the Society the dispenser. Actually, each of his books which appeared yearly was a fresh revelation of some truth Jehovah had imparted to him. Systematically, he laid the foundation for his many-tiered salvation classes.

In Russell's last book, *The Finished Mystery,* which the Judge announced after his death, he identified the "Great Crowd," as well as the "Little Flock (the 144,000)," as heavenly groups. He also mentioned a third group, also spirit begotten (pp. 130-134). Under Rutherford's "new revelation" the "Great Multitude" became an earthly unregenerate class.

The "heavenly class" had two groups. The *Mordecai-Naomi Class* included the remnant of the 144,000 still on earth who made up the ruling class of the Society. Many of these became unfaithful and made up the "evil slave class." (They were mostly Russellites who dared question Rutherford.) Therefore, he came up with the *Ruth-Esther Class* who filled the vacancies left in the number 144,000. Later (1933) he classified the *Jonadab Class*, the "Great Multitude," who would serve God on earth without a new birth or being spirit filled. Demoting them from a "heavenly class" to an "earthly class" was imperative. With the remnant filled there was no room left for expansion. These Jonadabs were the "hewers of wood and the carriers of water" adapted from the slave relationship of the Gibeonites to Israel (Jos. 10:10-27). These were the ones the Society would train for their booksellers.

## THE PENNY REWARD

To give a cloak of scripturalness Rutherford turned to Matthew 20:1-6 and carried it to the extreme. This parable of the penny became his "added light." The Society was the "vineyard of God," and the 12 years between 1919 and 1931 (when the Jonadabs were named publicly) were the 12 hours of the parable. The workday had ended and it was now time for "That Faithful and Wise Steward" (Russell claimed *he* was that steward) to pay out the penny. With great fanfare

Rutherford paid it out in July 1931, in Columbus, Ohio. They now had a new name: JEHOVAH'S WITNESSES. That was the penny! They now went door to door, serving the Society exclusively, and their reward was the privilege of calling themselves Jehovah's Witnesses, a title belonging to the 144,000. To earn this honor they would "publish" Watch Tower books for the rest of their natural lives.

The groundwork was completed; the class structure was set. The Organization was off to a running start with many carrying their bright new penny, organizational salvation.

By 1938 another name change was added: The New World Society. Although it was new to the Jonadabs, evidence of it was seen as early as 1926 when he called the faithful a "New Nation." It was born in 1938, another major doctrinal switch.

In 1929 he wrote in his book *Life* that the first consideration is the certainty of the promises that Israel shall be returned to Palestine (p. 120). Two years later he wrote in *Vindication,* "The literal promises made to national Israel are set aside and a spiritual application substituted." It's amazing what progressive revelation can do, isn't it? Israel is now rejected and the Society comes forth as the true Israel of God, or more perfectly: "The New World Society of Jehovah's Witnesses."

## TROUBLE IN THE NEW KINGDOM

Like Russell, the Kingdom's Director didn't have an easy road. In his book *Why Serve Jehovah,* Rutherford, like his predecessor, claimed to be the mouthpiece for God during his age. As President, he was the Director of Jehovah's visible Kingdom on earth, while the Society acts as the administrator of God's affairs.

Imagine his surprise when a mortal human sued the Kingdom for libel and won. Olin Moyle had been part of the movement for some 20 years, part of the time as head of the legal staff. But in 1939 Rutherford had him excommunicated from the Milwaukee congregation. In August of the next year, he was publicly discredited before 65,000 Witnesses in convention in St. Louis. In the heated aftermath, Rutherford made some false accusations in *The Watchtower;* so Moyle sued and was awarded $15,000.00 in 1914. Can you imagine someone successfully suing Jehovah's Kingdom of Truth for false statements and winning?

Rutherford was an angry man who spent his life openly attacking religion, politics, and commerce with some rugged language. His book *Enemies* says, "All liars and murderers are religionists" (p. 118). "Satan's Organization includes all Christendom, both Catholic, Protestant, liberal and conservative." "All religion is a racket and a snare" *(Religion,* p. 104). Perhaps the most livid example of his anger is in his book *Enemies:*

"Religion, religious organizations, and practitioners of religion (in these . . . are included thieves, robbers, liars, whoremongers, murderers, man-stealers or kidnappers, frauds, cheats . . . etc.); and all such like . . . and using a great mountain of lies behind which the rackateers hide themselves" (p. 306).

His attitude toward anything anti-Watchtower was so hate-filled and outspoken that in 1940 *The Saturday Evening Post* published an article called "Jehovah's Witnesses Make Hate A Religion."

## HOW DID HE SUCCEED?

It's obvious his legal mind and training helped. Regardless of his false prophecies he united the disconnected units into a Theocratic Organization. As new people came into the movement he held them spellbound with his oratory coupled with the expectancy of prophecies yet to be fulfilled. For the most part they were disgusted people who found in the Judge an outlet for their hostility toward political rulers. But perhaps the real reason is a human failing. Most people refuse to think for themselves and like Russell, Rutherford depended on the principle that if you say something often and long enough people will eventually accept it. Some 300 million copies of his writings were circulated. He successfully implanted Theocratic Consciousness and fear. Fear of leaving the Society, fear of disapproval, fear of all outside churches (all clergy are antichrist), fear of believing a false prophet or the devil (always found outside the Organization), and of course, the fear of Armageddon. They must depend on the Society for their "spiritual food" and "light."

He organized a Society of slaves!

## CHAPTER 9 – HAVE THEY CHANGED? I HAVEN'T MET ONE LIKE HIM.

They have changed, not doctrinally, but in their public image. After the Judge's death in 1942, the Society found fresh, dynamic leadership in Nathan Knorr, Rutherford's bodyguard. Born in 1905 in Bethlehem, Pennsylvania, he became associated with the Watch Tower at 16, and resigned his membership in the Reformed Church. After completing high school in 1923, he became a full-time minister and staff member in Brooklyn. He agreed with Rutherford in 1927 and suggested they dismiss the public meeting and have a one-hour canvassing drive instead. By 1932 he was General Manager of the publishing house; two years later he was elected to the New York Corporation Board of Directors, and he was finally elected President in 1942.

### THE TEACHER

Obviously learning from the mistakes of his predecessor, he continued the steady flow of literature, but without the author's name – giving it an illusion of spirituality and mystery. At least the actual writer was free from public criticism. Because he regarded his particular administration as one emphasizing education, I've titled him "THE TEACHER."

To improve their public image he replaced the phonograph-carrying debaters of Rutherford's era with Witnesses who were trained both in doctrine and presentation. It worked! When he took over there were less than 200,000 Witnesses; today there are more than 1½ million.

In 1943 he opened the first Gilead Bible School at the Kingdom Farm in South Lansing, New York. (The Kingdom Farm is where much of the food is grown to feed the publishing house and factory workers who work for $14.00 a month.) Two five-month classes a year were conducted, but in 1961 the school was transferred to the Brooklyn facility and a ten-month crash program begun.

Also in 1943, he inaugurated the Theocratic Ministry School in the Kingdom Halls, where every Witness is perpetually trained in the art of public speaking, sermon preparation, and placing the Society's literature. In 1958 women were allowed to participate in the School, not as public speakers, but in demonstrating the door-to-door witnessing methods.

By 1946 it was evident Mr. Knorr was also a brilliant administrator. He overhauled the district arrangements by replacing the zone with circuit work and reorganized the semi-annual assemblies. In 1950 123,000 followers met in Yankee Stadium; nearly 165,000 in 1953; and by 1958 both Yankee Stadium and the Polo Grounds overflowed with more than a quarter million people. The 1969 International Assembly of Jehovah's Witnesses was held in both the United States and Europe with over 840,000 attending.

Gradually the central control, with a complete top-down control, was perfected. Committees of three were appointed by Headquarters in each Kingdom Hall to do the Society's bidding, disfellowshipping at will, often sentencing whole families and innocent children to perish at Armageddon. They were necessary, they claimed, to keep the Organization pure.

The year 1950 marked a major milestone in Knorr's educational program. Until that time the "ministers" frequently found themselves embarrassed when their doctrinal aberrations were challenged by the Greek Scriptures. To solve the problem, the Society brought forth its own translation, *The New World Translation,* purposely defending their doctrines.

This wasn't publicly admitted until *The Watchtower* (12/63) confessed: "Among the various other ways in which *The New World Translation* honors God is by keeping clear from trinitarian bias. THAT IS WHY IT RENDERS THE CONTROVERSIAL PHRASE OF JOHN 1:1, 'The Word was a god . . . ' " The same way Russell and Rutherford crystallized their doctrines in their books, the Society deliberately juggled the Greek text, not because it warranted it, but to STAY CLEAR OF TRINITARIAN BIAS.

*The Kingdom Interlinear Translation of the Greek Scriptures* appeared in 1969, marking an end to *The Emphatic Diaglott* which had suffered from public criticism for years. The literal translation of the Greek text compared with the NWT in the margin is a jewel for exposing the errors existing in the 1950 edition of the NWT.

Other changes are evident too. Religion was once a dirty word, as was denomination, but the Society now claims to be a religion and a denomination. "Companies" have become congregations; "publishers," the door-to-door book placer-salesmen, are now ministers; "company servants" are now presiding ministers. Where they once met in rented halls or private homes, they now have their own Kingdom Halls, modest but adequate.

The perennial problem of the "ancient worthies" appearing back on earth before Armageddon was solved by Knorr in 1950. Basing his progressive revelation on Psalm 45:16, he discovered that "your sons shall be appointed in place of the fathers." Therefore, members of the Society today can become "princes" on the earth. No new birth is required, much less being spirit baptized or partakers of the heavenly nature, yet they can be accepted, "not in the spirit plane of being, but to the earthly plane. Such would come in under the same conditions as the ancient worthies who were accepted of God." That settled that! Wonder what happened to the

Judge's revelation and "added light"?

Truth never changes! Our understanding is improved, but the content remains the same, without change. Such cannot be said for the "added light" of the Society.

What began when a teen-ager rebelled against the Word as written, explored the mystical oriental religions, and finally settled on Adventism from which he created his private religion, has grown tier by tier. Regardless of the denial, the Watch Tower Foundation *is* Russell and his "logic of infidelity."

When Rutherford became President he replaced much of Russell's ideas with his own. And now, a new, yet another gospel is taught. When Rutherford died, new books, rubber-stamped by the Society, provided yet another gospel. In less than three short generations Russell's "reasonings" became Rutherford's "policies" and finally Knorr's "teachings," having gone through three changes.

Truth never changes.

Are these people Christian?

Let's take a look at what they actually teach and believe.

# II

## THE GOSPEL OF THE WATCH TOWER

"Any fair person can agree that Jehovah's Witnesses are better qualified to state the facts from the record than one who opposes them," they write. So on compliance with their request I'll let their records provide this theological statement taken directly from their books in context.

**CHAPTER 10 – GOD: Jehovah is the greatest personality in the universe, distinguished by that exclusive name *(Make Sure of All Things,* p. 188).**

1. He is not a triune god, which false doctrine would deny His almighty supremacy *(Ibid.,* p. 188).
2. There was . . . a time when Jehovah was all alone in the universal space. Then the time came when Jehovah began to create *(New Heavens and New Earth,* p. 14).
3. He is not omnipresent, but His power extends everywhere *(Make Sure of All Things,* p. 191).
4. His vindication is more important than the salvation of men. Since vindication of Jehovah's name and sovereignty is the foremost doctrine of the Bible, his name and kingdom find first place in the model prayer *(Let God Be True,* pp. 29, 163).

**CHAPTER 11 – JESUS CHRIST, a created individual, is the second greatest Personage in the universe.**

A. HIS PRE-EXISTENCE

1. There was a time when Jesus was *not.* Until His first

creation Jehovah God was sonless; by it He became a Father *(New Heavens and New Earth,* p. 24).

2. Michael the archangel is no other than the only begotten Son of God, now Jesus Christ *(Ibid.,* p. 30).

3. He is also God's "only begotten" Son, in that he is the only one directly created by Jehovah God *(The Truth That Leads to Eternal Life,* p. 47).

4. Thus he ranked with God's creation, being first among them and also most beloved and favored among them. After God had *created* him as His firstborn Son, then God *used* him as His working Partner in creating of all the rest of creation *(Let God Be True,* p. 33).

5. Although Logos was "a god," he did not think himself co-equal with Jehovah God; he did not view himself as equal in power with Jehovah God; he did not view himself as equal in glory *(Ibid.,* p. 37).

B. HIS INCARNATION AND HUMAN EXISTENCE

1. Jesus' birth was *not* an incarnation . . . He was flesh *(What Has Religion Done for Mankind?* p. 321).

2. Jesus was *not* a divine being on earth, although having a heavenly past and background *(The Kingdom Is at Hand,* p. 49).

3. His spirit existence *ended* when he was born a human and for 30 years he was an ex-son of God on probation *(The Word, Who Is He?* p. 11). He was *not* one with the Father in essence and nature, but they were one by being in agreement with each other as Father and Son *(Ibid.,* p. 30).

4. The primary purpose of the Son of God in coming to earth was to meet and decisively answer Satan's charge and vindicate His Father's name, and prove His worthiness to be the seed or the King of God's capital organization. The secondary purpose was, namely, to die as a holy sacrifice to Jehovah God in order to cancel death's condemnation *(What Has Religion Done for Mankind,* pp. 240-245).

5. By his water baptism Jesus showed his submitting of himself to do God's will . . . God begat Jesus to be his spiri-

tual Son *once more* instead of a human Son. By being thus anointed with the Spirit Jesus *became* the Messiah *(Let God Be True,* p. 38).

C. HIS RANSOM DEATH

1. That which is redeemed or brought back is what was lost, namely, *perfect human life,* with its rights and earthly prospects *(Let God Be True,* p. 114).

2. Jesus' blood spilled in death, his human life poured out in willing sacrifice, this is what the ransom is. It was not taken back by Jesus at his resurrection, for he was raised a divine spirit creature *(Ibid.,* p. 116).

3. Jesus' ransom is only for the *many,* not for everyone who has lived. Salvation is for "men of all kinds," not every last one who has lived. God selects those who receive salvation. Others have *no* hope of life *(Make Sure of All Things,* pp. 334, 336).

D. HIS RESURRECTION

1. He was put to death a man, but was raised from the dead a spirit being of the highest order . . . *the man Jesus is dead, forever dead (Studies in the Scriptures,* Vol. V, pp. 453, 454).

2. Our Lord's human body was removed from the tomb by the power of God. . . . The Scripture does not reveal what became of the body except that it did not decay or corrupt *(The Harp of God,* p. 170).

3. Resurrection does *not* involve the restoring of the original body of the creature, but the soul is recreated *(Make Sure of All Things,* p. 311). It is the thought life and memory pattern that is remembered in resurrection *(Ibid.,* p. 311).

4. His body, flesh and bones, was given as a ransom, therefore it could not be resurrected or taken off God's altar. He was not given human life again, because that would have meant that he was taking back the ransom price *(The Watchtower,* 4/15, 1963).

5. He was re-created as a divine spirit creature *(Let God Be True,* p. 116).

## CHAPTER 12 – THE HOLY SPIRIT

It is God's active force, not Jehovah's power residing within Himself, but His energy when projected out from Himself. It is not a person, but is subject to God . . . it is at all times under His control . . . and therefore is likened to a radar beam *(Make Sure of All Things,* pp. 389, 432, 433).

A. BAPTISM IN THE HOLY SPIRIT

1. Baptism into the Body of Christ is for 144,000 *only* and done by baptizing them with the Holy Spirit *(Ibid.,* p. 34).

2. Only Christ and his 144,000 spiritual brothers can be born again and receive the spirit baptism which is for body members only *(Ibid.,* pp. 33, 49).

**CHAPTER 13 – WHAT IS MAN? Earthly souls, *human* or *animal,* have an organism of flesh kept living by means of blood circulating in their system *(Make Sure of All Things,* p. 349).**

1. Thus we learn that man is a combination of two things, namely, the "dust of the ground" and "the breath of life." The combining of these two things produced a living soul or creature called man *(Let God Be True,* p. 68).

2. So we see that the claim of religionists that man was an immortal soul and therefore differs from the beast is not Scriptural *(Ibid.,* p. 68).

3. . . . even the man Christ Jesus was mortal. He did not have an immortal soul: Jesus, the human soul, died. Immortality is a reward for faithfulness. It does not come automatically to a human at birth *(Ibid.,* pp. 71, 74).

**CHAPTER 14 – THE COMING OF CHRIST: The second presence *(parousia*-Greek), Matthew 24:3, of Christ the Messiah was to be invisible and unmistakable sign he gave shows**

**conclusively that this return of Christ *began* in 1914 *(Make Sure of All Things,* p. 319).**

1. The purpose of his second presence requires it to be invisible, but by the sign given he appears to the eyes of the understanding . . . *(This Means Everlasting Life,* p. 215).

2. For many years prior to 1914 earnest Bible students understood that the year 1914 marked the *end* of the Gentile times. *That* date marked the beginning of the "time of the end" of Satan's rule, and therefore the time when Christ Jesus the Righteous Ruler of the new world received control *(Ibid.,* p. 201).

3. In the autumn of 1914 he came to the spiritual temple as Jehovah's Messenger and began to cleanse it. So this occurred in the spring of 1918. Since 1914 the present Christ has been making the evidences of his second presence or *parousia* manifest.

4. Since World War I this witness to the established Kingdom has been preached to all nations without letup. Acceptance of the reigning King and his kingdom is the only security for anyone *(Ibid.,* pp. 201, 202, 222, 204).

**CHAPTER 15 – THE RESURRECTION OF MANKIND is the restoration of the nonexistent dead. It is the reactivating of the life pattern of the creature, and is referred to as being in His memory. Resurrection does not involve the restoring of the original identical body of the creature *(Make Sure of All Things,* p. 311).**

1. The life pattern is restored . . . the mental abilities, memory growth and his characteristics. Only those in God's memory have hope; the wicked will never be remembered for resurrection *(Ibid.,* pp. 311, 314).

2. The 144,000 sharing in Christ's death are raised to heaven to share in the first resurrection . . . which took place in 1918 *(Ibid.,* pp. 315, 316).

3. Since all the members of Christ's body had not died before 1918, those of the "remnant" receive an immediate change to "spirit life" when they die *(Let God Be True,* pp. 203, 278).

4. Faithful other sheep dying now have hope of resurrection *on* earth *(Ibid.,* p. 317).

5. The resurrection of people, the unrighteous as well as the righteous, *will not mean their final salvation.* It will merely open up to them an opportunity for everlasting salvation *(The Watchtower,* 3/16/65, p. 179).

6. There will be an earthly resurrection (the first resurrection is spiritual and applies to Christ and the 144,000). It will include those who "did good things," those of the "other sheep" class who may die now before the war of Armageddon. On the other hand, "those who practiced vile things" are those who have no faith and knowledge of God and who have done wrong because of being ignorant. . . . After being raised from the tombs they do not participate in bringing forth children, but Jesus' words at Luke 20:34-36 show their opportunity *(Ibid.,* p. 280).

**CHAPTER 16 – SIN: There are two kinds of sin.**

1. Inherited, which does not incur death, i.e., from which there is hope of being released;

2. Willful, which brings a sentence of everlasting destruction.

3. Only inherited sins are *excused* by Jesus' sacrifice.

4. Sinless mankind will meet the mark of perfection at the end of the 1,000 year reign *(Make Sure of All Things,* pp. 344, 347).

**CHAPTER 17 – THE KINGDOM is the Sovereign empowered Theocratic government. It is comprised of the King Christ Jesus and 144,000 associate kings taken from among**

**men. This Kingdom began operation in full power with the enthronement of Christ in the heavens, A.D. 1914 *(Make Sure of All Things,* p. 226).**

1. The Revelation limits to 144,000 the number that become a part of the kingdom and stand on heavenly Mount Zion *(Let God Be True,* p. 136).

2. Since 1914 . . . Christ Jesus began to rule in the midst of his enemies *(Ibid.,* p. 138). The undefeatable purpose of Jehovah God to establish a righteous Kingdom in these last days was fulfilled in A.D. 1914 *(Ibid.,* p. 143). (Note: That Kingdom is the Watch Tower Society.)

3. This is not the good news (gospel) of a kingdom coming, but the news of one *now* established. So from and after 1919 the most sustaining publicity campaign ever given on earth has been to the effect that "the kingdom of the heavens has drawn near" *(Ibid.,* p. 141).

**CHAPTER 18 – ARMAGEDDON, THE LAST WAR: The battle of Jehovah God the Almighty . . . to destroy Satan and his demonic and human organization *(Make Sure of All Things,* p. 24).**

1. Christ returns . . . to put all enemies under his feet at Armageddon. By clearing out false religion, by restoring true worship, and by re-establishing the divine government toward the earth *(Let God Be True,* p. 206).

2. Armageddon will begin just after Satan attacks the Society. Gog the Devil uses the nations and rulers of the earth to attack the New World Society *(From Paradise Lost,* p. 206).

3. All those outside the New World Society will perish with Satan and his demons. More than two billion will die *(You Must Survive Armageddon Into God's New World,* p. 341).

4. The undedicated children (Note: Those not baptized as Witnesses) of goatish people will *not* be spared from execu-

tion and being sentenced to Gehenna, just because they are themselves minor, unresponsible children *(The Watchtower,* 3/15/65, p. 176).

5. According to this trustworthy Bible chronology six thousand years from man's creation will end in 1975, and the seventh period of a thousand years of human history will begin in the fall of 1975 *(Life Everlasting, in Freedom of the Sons of God*, p. 29).

## CHAPTER 19 – SALVATION AND THE NEW BIRTH is *either* to a heavenly life or an earthly life on earth.

A. THE LITTLE FLOCK

1. Only these 144,000 can be born again, be spirit baptized, partakers of the Divine nature and have a heavenly hope *(This Means Everlasting Life,* pp. 114-117).

2. They must sacrifice their human lives in God's service, forever giving up the prospect of living as human creatures perfected in the righteous new world *(Ibid.,* p. 120).

3. Persons thus justified are declared righteous *in order to be sacrificed* with Christ and have hope of heavenly life *(Ibid.,* p. 120). (Note: Because they don't believe in Jesus' bodily resurrection and to quiet His words in John 2:18-21 they are forced to make the "body" in verse 21 mean the Church Body. Therefore the remnant or the 144,000 also BECOME PART OF CHRIST'S SACRIFICE, being part of the ransom. In other words, the 144,000 become part of the sin offering!)

B. THE GREAT CROWD

1. An unnumbered crowd of faithful persons now working as Jehovah's Witnesses are sometimes called His "other sheep" or "Jonadabs." They do not expect to go to heaven. They have been promised everlasting life on earth *(Let God Be True,* p. 231).

2. Not that they are at present justified by God for their

faith to be acceptable for sacrifice with Christ in his death; but that they, in faith, have taken the right attitude toward Jehovah's King and have acted right toward the King's brothers (Note: The living 144,000 still on earth) *(This Means Everlasting Life,* p. 242).

3. Salvation to life involves time and is *not* completed when one becomes a Christian *(Make Sure of All Things,* p. 332).

4. Salvation "by means of" or from Armageddon disaster is based on a baptism into Christ Jesus. They are conducting themselves in holy acts of conduct and deeds of godly devotion and are waiting the world's end *(Ibid.,* p. 266). (Note: Salvation is not from sin but from Armageddon in order to receive a *chance* for 1,000 years of probation proving themselves worthy of life.)

5. To come under Jehovah's good will we must:

a. Take in knowledge. With God's word in our heads, we have a new force to dictate the law of our mind *(Let God Be True,* p. 308).

b. Meet with other people who have this same knowledge and faith *(This Means Everlasting Life,* p. 312). (Note: This is important because this "truth" can come only through studying Watchtower study guides.)

c. We must also publicly declare the Kingdom to others *(Ibid.,* p. 243).

d. Imitate Jesus by dedicating ourselves in baptism *(From Paradise Lost,* pp. 242-249).

**CHAPTER 20 – CONGREGATION OF GOD: The "holy nation" is comprised of Jesus Christ, the Head, and 144,000 members of His body *(Make Sure of All Things,* p. 70).**

1. This congregation, then, is restricted to this select, predestined number; and in heaven it is made the capital part or ruling body of Jehovah's universal organization *(Let God Be True,* p. 130).

2. God began raising the temple body on the third day *(Ibid.,* p. 389). (Note: Again we see their attempt to explain away the bodily resurrection of Jesus. That the church didn't come into existence until the Day of Pentecost, 50 days later, doesn't deter them.)

3. The 144,000 sharing in Christ's death are raised to heaven to share in the first resurrection. The earlier ones of the 144,000 slept in death until the day of Christ's manifestation, A.D. 1918 *(Ibid.,* pp. 315, 316).

4. Proving itself thus to be a "faithful and discreet slave," the remnant was approved by the returned Lord Jesus Christ, who then did as he had foretold in Matthew 24:47. This worldwide care of the Kingdom interests is being carried on under the supervision of the Watch Tower Bible and Tract Society of Pennsylvania, with which the governing body of Jehovah's Witnesses is connected *(The Watchtower,* 7/1/20, pp. 195-200).

**CHAPTER 21 – JUDGMENT: This is simply a trial of life. It is not to be feared or dreaded. It is the first thousand years of the new world *(Let God Be True,* p. 286). The unjust, the ignorant and unrighteous will rise from the grave and will be given their guaranteed chance to obey the gospel and be saved *(The Watchtower,* 3/15/65, p. 178).**

1. In the spring of 1918 he (Jesus) came as Jehovah's Messenger to the temple (the 144,000 remnant of Witnesses) and began judgment first of the "house of God" (which resulted in the expulsion eventually of more than 40,000 Russellites who rejected Rutherford's doctrines), and then of the nations of the world, separating them like sheep and goats *(Let God Be True,* p. 287).

2. Though many are not aware of it, that separation is now going on. One's attitude toward the remnant of Jehovah's anointed witnesses and the message of his Theocratic government reveals one's attitude toward Jehovah's installed King

*(Ibid.,* p. 204).

3. Not all persons who have lived and died on the earth during the past six thousand years will come forth to judgment in this judgment day. Others who will not come forth are those religionists who Jesus said could not escape the judgment of Gehenna because of being the seed of the serpent *(Ibid.,* p. 289).

**CHAPTER 22 – HELL: The false conception of eternal torment after death was introduced early into apostate Christianity, and by the fourth century after Christ was firmly entrenched in false religion. It is based on Satan's original lie in Eden *(Make Sure of All Things,* p. 155).**

1. Hell is . . . a God dis-honoring doctrine *(Let God Be True,* p. 88).

2. The doctrine of a burning hell where the wicked are *tortured* eternally after death cannot be true, mainly for the four reasons: (1) it is wholly unscriptural; (2) it is unreasonable; (3) it is contrary to God's love; and (4) it is repugnant to justice *(Ibid.,* p. 99).

3. It is so plain that the Bible hell is mankind's common grave that even an honest little child can understand it *(Ibid.,* p. 92).

4. So the everlasting punishment of the "goats" is their everlasting being cut off from all life *(Ibid.,* p. 89).

**CHAPTER 23 – CHARISMATA OR GIFTS FROM GOD**

1. The purpose of the miraculous gifts given to the early Christian congregation is to establish and mature the congregation and show a change from dealing with the old system of things to the new Christian system *(Make Sure of All Things,* p. 137).

2. So when the Christian congregation grew to adulthood,

that is, reached maturity by becoming a recognized, established organization, these miraculous gifts passed away *(The Watchtower,* 6/1/63, p. 343).

3. Therefore, when the apostles died, and when those who had received the miraculous gifts through them passed from the earthly scene, the supernatural gifts of the spirit, including speaking in tongues, ceased *(Ibid.,* p. 343).

4. Divine physical healing is not experienced today, since special gifts passed away after the death of the apostles. Healing and other gifts passed on only by the apostles or in their presence *(Make Sure of All Things,* pp. 145, 149).

5. Since the Scriptures clearly show that it is not God's spirit then it is an instance of the operation of Satan and his demons. Those who seek these miraculous gifts that God no longer bestows upon his people lend themselves to such deception by Satan *(The Watchtower,* 6/1/63, p. 344).

**CHAPTER 24 – EXTRA-BIBLICAL INSPIRATION: "All Bible translations and interpretations emanate from God. They are passed to the Holy Spirit who invisibly communicated with Jehovah's Witnesses – and the publicity department" according to F.W. Frantz, Vice-President *(Scottish Daily Press,* Nov. 24, 1954, reporting Frantz' court testimony).**

1. . . . that he and N.H. Knorr head the secret translation committee of seven . . . that Knorr and Frantz, not the Committee, have the last word. This is accomplished by "angels of different ranks who control Witnesses."

2. Note: Frantz was in Scotland convincing the courts the Society was another denomination, hoping its ministers would be granted military deferment. After 80 years of preaching denominationalism was anti-God, he went to great lengths to prove they were really "just another denomination."

Secondly: they departed from the logical, "Let-us-reason-together" approach and admitted to some sort of angelic revelationary process. After working with this Greek translation and pointing out many glaring errors (and I'm not a Greek scholar, only a student), the angels finally returned for additional study. Of late, they've discarded *The Emphatic Diaglott* for a standard *Wescott and Hort* Greek text, and the new *Kingdom Interlinear* translation reveals the angels apparently changed their minds.

**CHAPTER 25 – THE PROPHET AND DATE SETTING: In the April 1, 1972 *Watchtower* article, "They Shall Know That A Prophet Was Among Them," the Society, as Jehovah's earthly Organization, lays claim to being "the prophet."**

1. This "prophet" was not one man, but was a body of men and women. Today they are known as Jehovah's Christian witnesses *(The Watchtower,* 7/1/74, p. 401). . . . from the time of its organization (1884) until now the Lord has used it as His channel through which to make known the Glad Tidings *(The Watch Tower,* p. 22, 1917, quoted in *The Finished Mystery).*

2. The following excerpts are examples of the "changing times and dates" "the prophet" dispenses. Deuteronomy 18:20-22 says that the prophet whose words fail to take place is not to be feared or heeded.

a. In 1889 Russell wrote in *The Time Is at Hand,* p. 101, "The setting up of the Kingdom of God is already begun, and that Armageddon will end in A.D. 1915 with the complete overthrow of earth's present rulership."

b. We see no reason for changing the figures. . . . They are, we believe, God's dates, not ours. But bear in mind that the *end* of 1914 is . . . the *end* of the time of trouble *(Watch Tower Reprints II,* p. 1677).

c. *The Finished Mystery,* released posthumously as Russell's last volume after his death in 1916, changed the dates scheduled to expire in 1914 to 1918-1925 as Rutherford took up the prophet's mantle.

Some interesting developments . . . with the setting up of the Kingdom may occur in 1920, six years after the Great Time of Trouble began. (Note: Russell said the Time would END in 1914 not BEGIN.) . . . and that the "fire" will come in the fall of 1920 (this was "changed" in the 1926 edition to read, "and that the 'fire' will follow in due course") (p. 178).

d. Rutherford claimed in *Millions Now Living Will Never Die,* p. 97, that "1925 shall mark the resurrection of the faithful worthies of old." When 1925 came he was proven a false prophet.

e. By 1929 he changed his issue from the 1925 failure to "If the end of 1925 marks the end of the last fifty-year period . . . we should expect . . . to receive some knowledge concerning God's great plan of restoration. The Jews are to have the favors first" *(Life,* p. 170). The premise that the natural Jews would return to Palestine was discarded a year or two later. Israel today is the Society and its faithful followers.

f. In 1931 he wrote in *Vindication,* Vol. 1, pp. 338, 339, "There was a measure of disappointment . . . concerning the years 1914, 1918 and 1925. Later the faithful learned that these dates were definitely fixed in the Scriptures; and THEY ALSO LEARNED TO QUIT FIXING DATES FOR THE FUTURE AND PREDICTING WHAT WOULD COME TO PASS ON A CERTAIN DATE."

g. But by 1942 we see a shift again, back to date setting. In 1943, *The Trust Shall Make You Free* cautioned: "The final war will come as a sudden and complete surprise. We are therefore near the end of six thousand years of human history . . . " (pp. 152, 341). "The disaster of Armageddon . . . is at the door" *(Let God Be True,* p. 194).

h. In 1966 a new date for the completion of 6,000 years of human existence and government was calculated. "Six thousand years from man's creation will end in 1975, and the seventh period of a thousand years of human history will begin in the fall of 1975 C.E." *(Life Everlasting – In Free-*

*dom of the Sons of God,* p. 29).

i. That a dual system of dates is possible is seen in the fact that although certain dates – and doctrines – had been changed, books containing the "old" errors were still sold. For several years after Rutherford's death his books were sold. *Life,* (1929) said that Israel would be returned to Palestine, a doctrine the Society changed in 1930. *The Harp of God* (1921) taught Russell's chronology that the "end" began in 1799 and the "Lord's presence dates from 1874," even though the Society now dates the Presence from 1914-1918. He taught that the "great crowd" was a Spirit-begotten class *(Vindication,* 1932). Many years after the Society had reversed itself it sold these books, apparently to get the revenue from them.

j. Changing dates, changing doctrines, changing salvation, all the work of "the prophet." Does God change His mind? "If a prophet speak and it does not come to pass he speaks presumptuously. He is not to be feared!"

# BIBLE ANSWERS FOR WATCHTOWER QUESTIONS

## CHAPTER 26 – HOW CAN I HELP THEM? THEY CONFUSE ME!

Keep in mind that all dedicated Witnesses have already settled their minds that all other beliefs "are of the devil." This attitude, motivated by the fear of Armageddon, doesn't make it easy but there is one thing going for them. They'll accept the Scripture as full and final authority once they see the truth so use it freely for their spiritual welfare.

Their problem is basically a Jesus problem. Satan's attack on the Person of Christ has always been His identity. It's the "spirit of Antichrist." The seven major doctrines which all Witnesses must teach are basically attacks or denials of the Person and claims of Christ Jesus.

1. Jesus is "a god" *therefore* . . .

2. Jesus is an angel, a secondary god, so man isn't created in his image.

3. Jesus' death was primarily for vindication of Jehovah's name; secondly, for man's sin. There was no incarnation so wrath of God is not of primary importance.

4. Jesus was not raised bodily.

5. If Jesus is only an angel He can't indwell the believer.

1. There is no Trinity or equality.

2. Man has no immortal "inner man."

3. There is no Bible hell, therefore man can prove himself worthy or earn his own salvation.

4. There is no visible second coming.

5. No new birth is necessary except for the 144,000,

| | |
|---|---|
| | a denial of personal salvation. |
| 6. There is no bodily resurrection. | 6. Jesus came secretly in 1914 resulting in "another gospel" about an established kingdom. |
| 7. He returned invisibly in 1914. | 7. This robs Him of His majesty as King of Kings, and allows the Watch Tower Society to rule in His place. |

## CHAPTER 27 – IS GOD A TRINITY?

Scripture reveals the Supreme Being, Who is Spirit, as Father, Son, and Holy Spirit. One can readily distinguish three manifestations or personalities, who are not three gods in one, yet they appear as equal and eternal.

If it can be demonstrated from the New Testament that there are three persons who are all called God and Jehovah, and then shown there is only one God, Jehovah, there is only one conclusion, these three personalities must be God. "Things being equal to the same thing are equal to each other."

### GOD THE FATHER

In 2 Peter 1:17 the identity of two persons is seen; one called "God the father," the other "the beloved Son." There isn't any problem as to Who God the Father is; He is Jehovah God.

1. God is *not* a solitary Being, but a composite unity. "Jehovah our God is one *(echod)* Jehovah." The word one, *echod,* doesn't mean an absolute unity – that word would be *yachid* (see Ezra 2:64 for example). In Genesis 2:24 God said, "Let them become one *(echod)* flesh," and 1:15: "Day and night are one *(echod)* day." It took one man and one woman, one day and one night to make one flesh and one

day, yet both are distinguishable and separate.

2. The plural noun *Elohim* is used for God and always with a plural verb. If it meant "majesty" as when used for Kings as the Witnesses explain, the verb would be singular. The Kings of Israel, however, are never addressed except in the singular. Therefore, the usage of the plural noun and verb are in agreement with the Deuteronomy 6:4 truth that God is a unity.

3. This is borne out again when Jehovah refers to Himself using plural pronouns. "Let *us* make man in *our* image after *our* likeness" (Gen. 1:26, NWT). The Witness reply that God was conversing with his helper-creator, Michael-Jesus, begs the question. Was man created in the image of God or the image of the angel of God? If this plurality denotes Majesty, was Jesus the Creator, as Paul states in Colossians 1:16, or Jehovah? Since there is *no* other God (Isa. 43:10), Jehovah must have been addressing a co-equal Godhead!

4. The manifestations of Jehovah were frequently triune. In Genesis 18:2 Jehovah appeared to Abraham on the plains of Mamre with two angels: " . . . he looked and there were three men." In verse 3 he addressed *them* (all three) as Jehovah as though they were all one. And in verse 9 "they" spoke to him as one voice: "Then Jehovah said to Abraham . . . " Fourteen times Abraham spoke to "them" as Jehovah.

5. In Genesis 19:24 we read: "Then Jehovah made it rain sulphur and fire upon Sodom and Gomorrah from Jehovah out of heaven." Unquestionably, Jehovah God the Father in heaven rained down fire, while Jehovah God the Son was on the earth.

## GOD THE SON

1. ARE THERE ANY NEW TESTAMENT REFERENCES WHERE JESUS IS CALLED JEHOVAH AND GOD?

a. In Revelation 1:8 we read, "I am the Alpha and Omega, says Jehovah God, the One who is and who was and who is coming, the Almighty God" (NWT). The Watchtower

Bible identifies the one speaking as Jehovah.

b. Turning to chapter 22:7 the One speaking says, "I am coming quickly," and again in verse 12: "Look! I am coming quickly, I am the Alpha and the Omega, the first and the last, the beginning and the end." By cross-referencing with Revelation 1:8 we can identify the speaker as Jehovah the Almighty.

c. In Revelation 22:16 the One speaking says, "I Jesus have sent my angel . . . " and again in 22:20: "Surely I am coming quickly, Amen." The One coming quickly in 22:7 is the same one in verse 12 who is the Alpha and Omega of verse 13, identified in 1:8 as Jehovah God the Almighty. Now back to 22:20: "Amen! Come, Lord Jesus."

d. The Alpha and Omega of 22:13 is the First and the Last of 1:17 who is Jesus in 1:18. But lest you feel this identification is insufficient turn to Isaiah 44:6: "Thus saith Jehovah . . . I am the first, and I am the last, and beside me there is no God." The identity is irrefutable. Either there are two firsts and lasts (which would be linguistic suicide) and there are two Alpha and Omega (which would be Greek confusion) or they are the same Person.

e. In Revelation 1:8 the Alpha and Omega was also identified as the one who was, and is, and is coming. By comparing Matthew 24:30 we discover the *only* one coming in clouds is Jesus.

f. There are a number of New Testament passages which refer directly to Christ, in which the Old Testament calls Him Jehovah. Matthew 3:3; Mark 1:2, 3; Luke 3:4; and John 1:23 all quote Isaiah 40:3: "Listen! Someone is calling you in the wilderness: 'Clear up the way of Jehovah, you people! Make the highway for our God through the desert plain straight!' " (NWT). Every Christian knows that this Herald was John the Baptist preparing the way for Jesus.

g. Compare Hebrews 1:10-12 (addressed to Jesus) with Psalm 102:24-27 which is addressed to Jehovah.

h. 1 Peter 2:3 quotes from Psalm 34:8 and clearly identifies Christ as Jehovah.

i. Isaiah 6:1, 3, 10 reports Isaiah's vision of the glory of Jehovah, while John 12:37-41 applies it to the glory of Christ.

j. The Apostle Paul had no problem with the identity of Jesus. He quotes Isaiah 45:23 in Philippians 2:10; Joel 2:32 in Romans 10:23, and Isaiah 45:23 again in Romans 14:11. In each Old Testament passage Jehovah is mentioned and Paul identifies Him as Jesus.

2. "The Mighty God in Isaiah 9:6 proves Jesus' secondary position," say the Witnesses, "because only Jehovah is Almighty." The title "Mighty God," however, is used for Jehovah in Jeremiah 32:18: "God, the great one, the mighty one *(el gibbor),* Jehovah of armies is His name." This title is used again in Isaiah 10:21. Are there two Mighty Gods?

3. Hebrews 1:6 and Luke 4:8 are two passages extremely upsetting to the Witnesses. In the Hebrews text Jehovah said, "Let all the angels worship Him!" and this is a direct command! Using the Watch Tower understanding the passage could read, "and let all the angels worship the chief angel, Michael." Jesus said in Luke 4:8, however, to "worship God and Him alone!" Apparently Jesus and His Father should get together! Unless we take Hebrews 1:8 exactly as written, the Father called His Son God.

a. The question in verse 5 *must* be answered. "Which of the angels were ever called, 'My Son,' I have begotten thee?" If Jesus was Michael, the chief angel, this question is irrelevant. If Jehovah did say to one particular angel, Michael, "You are my Son," the question is pointless. The truth is, Christ wasn't an angel. He said, "Worship God alone," and Jehovah said, "Let all the angels worship him, Jesus." The NWT rendering of verse 8, "God is your throne forever," is another example of deliberate tampering with the Greek text to serve their own ends. Note the exact meaning in *their* new *Kingdom Interlinear.*

4. The idea that Jehovah created Michael-Jesus in the beginning as a lesser god is totally unscriptural. There is only one God: "*Before* me there was *no* God formed (created),

and *after* me there continued to be none" (Isa. 43:10). This isn't an isolated passage. Isaiah 44:6 says, " . . . beside me there is no God." Verse 8: "Is there *a God* beside me? There is no God: I know not any" (45:18, 21; 46:9). If Jehovah created "another god" He didn't know anything about it. The united voice of the Scriptures stands solidly against the "two gods" of the Watchtower Society.

In Isaiah 43:11 we read, " . . . beside me there is no saviour." If there is only one saviour (see Isa. 45:21), and Jesus is the Name of the only Saviour (Acts 4:12), what is the only conclusion we can accept? They are one and the same! The truth contained in this passage forbids the Watchtower interpretation of Colossians 1:15, Revelation 3:14 and John 1:1.

There are three persons in the New Testament who are all called God and Jehovah.

## GOD THE HOLY SPIRIT

1. The Spirit is directly called God in Acts 5:4: " . . . thou hast not lied to men, but to God." In verse 3 Peter accused Ananias of "lying to the Holy Spirit." The Spirit in verse 3 is God in verse 4.

2. The Spirit is called Jehovah. By comparing Isaiah 6:8-10 with Acts 28:25-27, we see the consistency. Isaiah heard the voice of Jehovah while the Acts account says, "Well spake the Holy Spirit by Isaiah," quoting the same passage. More information will be supplied in the section dealing with the Holy Spirit, but we've accomplished what we set out to do. There are three persons all called God and Jehovah in the New Testament. However, 1 Timothy 2:5 declares there is only one God. The inescapable conclusion is they must be one and the same. We may not fully understand it with our finite minds but it's better to accept the record as written than deliberately twist the Scriptures as the Society has done in order to justify their understanding.

## CHAPTER 28 – IS THE HOLY SPIRIT A PERSON?

The Society has no difficulty acknowledging the personality of Satan and demons because they talk, plan, move, and feel as a person feels. Yet it goes out of its way to deny the personality of the Spirit even though the Spirit talks, feels, plans, moves, and can be grieved, quenched, and resisted. It can't be the absence of a body that hinders them. Neither Satan nor demons have bodies. Still, this active force, this nothingness, carries on the work of God according to their beliefs.

1. The Spirit is directly called God in Acts 5:3. Peter blames Ananias for deceiving the Holy Spirit, " . . . thou has not lied unto men, but unto God" (v. 4).

2. The Spirit is called Jehovah:

a. Exodus 17:2-7: " . . . because they tempted Jehovah." Yet the writer of Hebrews said, " . . . wherefore as the Holy Spirit said . . . when our fathers tempted me" (Heb. 3:7-9).

b. Compare Isaiah 6:8-10: " . . . also I heard the voice of Jehovah saying," with Acts 28:25-27: " . . . well spake the Holy Spirit by Esaias . . . "

c. Compare Jeremiah 31:34 with Hebrews 10:15-17. In each of these passages the Spirit of the New Testament is the Jehovah of the Old.

3. The Spirit is eternal and only God is eternal (Heb. 9:14; Ps. 90:2).

4. God *is* Spirit (John 4:24); there is only *one* Spirit (Eph. 4:4), who is the Spirit of the Lord (Isa. 40:13-14), and that Spirit IS the Lord (2 Cor. 3:17), Who is also called the Spirit of Christ (Rom. 8:9).

5. The Spirit was equal in authority with Jehovah in sending Christ to earth (Isa. 48:16).

6. The Spirit is omnipresent: "Whither shall I go from thy Spirit . . . whither shall I flee from thy presence?" (Ps. 139:7-10). The Jehovah's Witnesses teach that *God is not omnipresent.* However, if God isn't everywhere present at

once, and yet He was "in Christ reconciling the world unto himself" (2 Cor. 5:19), then at *that* time he must have been out of heaven and on earth. Or else, He IS omnipresent. The *New World Translation* insertion and addition of "by means of" in this text is purely arbitrary and unwarranted in the Greek.

7. The Spirit is omniscient: "Who hath directed the Spirit of the Lord, or being his counsellor hath taught him?" (Isa. 40:13, 14).

8. He is omnipotent: "But all these worketh that one and the self same Spirit dividing to every man severally as He will (1 Cor. 12:11).

9. The Spirit baptizes us into the Body of Christ (1 Cor. 12:13).

10. Jesus baptizes us into the Spirit; thence the Spirit manifests Himself through us supernaturally for service (1 Cor. 12:7-11).

11. The fruit of the Spirit is named in Galatians 5:22. These fruits are also the attributes of God.

12. The Spirit holds a unique position in the Godhead. All kinds of blasphemy against the Father and Son will be forgiven, but blasphemy against the Spirit is forever unforgivable (Matt. 12:31; Heb. 10:29).

13. Eventually the Jehovah's Witness will refer to the neuter pronoun "itself" and attempt to prove the Spirit is an "it," but this is easily answered. Greek grammar requires that pronouns agree with the antecedent in gender. *Pneuma* is a neuter noun meaning spirit but this doesn't warrant reducing Spirit to nothingness. In John 4:24, "God is spirit *(pneuma).*" Is God then an "it"? In Luke 1:35, Jesus is called "that holy thing" (neuter – it), yet we know He is a Person.

Where the pronoun *auto* (neuter) is used (John 14:17) the NWT renders it correctly as "it" to agree with the neuter noun, *pneuma.* But the Spirit of God as a Person is meant. Elsewhere, masculine pronouns are used for the Spirit. *Ekeinos* is rendered "that one" in the NWT but it should be more correctly "that man." Were the Spirit an "it" the pronoun *ekeino* (neuter) would have been used.

14. HOW COULD THE 120 PERSONS AT PENTECOST BE BAPTIZED WITH A PERSON? Can a Person be poured out on people? This question is supposed to bluff you but notice they weren't baptized *with* but *in* the Spirit. When the Greek word for Spirit is used more than 100 times *without* the article, it refers to the power of God; but when used *with* the article it speaks of the GIVER of power. They were immersed in the power of His Presence!

## CHAPTER 29 – IS JESUS A GOD, OR IS HE MICHAEL, THE ANGEL?

Jesus is Emmanuel – *with us is God* – the Bible's most important truth and Person, and can't be stressed with more emphasis than do His own words in Matthew 11:27: " . . . neither knoweth any man the Father, save the Son, and he to whomsoever the Son will reveal Him."

If Jesus is not God, then it is both blasphemy and idolatry to offer Him any type of worship. If He is God then He deserves, yea, He demands our worship. There are no degrees of Deity; either Christ is God or He isn't!

### HIS PRE-EXISTENCE

1. There are five favorite passages the Witnesses use to prove the creation of Jesus: Proverbs 8:22, 27-30; John 1:1-3; Philippians 2:5-8; Colossians 1:15-17 and Revelation 3:14.

2. Revelation 3:14 will probably be the first text they will turn to, " . . . the beginning of the creation of God." Colossians 1:15 states that He is "the firstborn of all creation." These texts supposedly prove that Jesus had a beginning, therefore He was created. Is this true?

a. The word "beginning" *(arche)* can be correctly rendered "origin" and is so translated in John 1:1 of the NWT.

*Thayer's Lexicon* gives the meaning not only as "beginning" and "origin," but also as "the person or thing that commences, that by which anything begins to be, the origin, active cause" (pp. 76, 77). Neither of these passages say Jesus is the "first" creation of God but the origin, the source out of which all creation flows. "Because IN HIM *(en auto)* was created all things, the things visible and the things invisible" *(The Kingdom Interlinear).*

This corroborates Hebrews 1:2 and Colossians 1:16, 17, confirming Christ as the Creator of all things and therefore God (Gen. 1:1). This is the reason the Translation Committee arbitrarily "added" *other* and *by means of* throughout the Colossians text. Their new *Kingdom Interlinear* repudiates this.

The Jehovah's Witnesses, in complete disregard for scholarship, stand completely alone in their dogmatic assertion on page 47 of the booklet *The Word, Who Is He?* that *arche* does not mean Beginner, Origin or Originator. *All* reputable scholars agree that *arche* always means source, first cause.

b. In Colossians 1:15-17, the Greek doesn't say Christ was created *by* God. The case is genitive which always means *of* God, never *by* God which would be instrumentative. The NWT in John 1:3 establishes Christ as the originator of everything. "Apart from him not even one thing came into existence." He created all; He began and completed all things. "All things were created *by* Him, and *for* him, and He is *before* all things, and *by* him all things consist."

c. In Hebrews 7:3 Melchisedec is compared with Jesus. "Without father, without mother, without descent, having neither beginning of days, nor end of life; but made *like unto* the Son of God." Can anything be more obvious? There isn't any record of Melchisedec's heritage, beginning or ending. Such a mystery is compared to Jesus, who also is without beginning or ending. He always was, the Alpha and Omega!

d. According to the prophet Micah, He is as eternal as the Father: "His going forth having been from everlasting."

The word "everlasting" is the same word used to show the eternal existence of Jehovah.

e. In John 17:5 Jesus prayed that the glory which He shared with the Father before the world was might be restored. This is enlightening when compared with Isaiah 42:8, where Jehovah said, " . . . and my glory I will *not* give to another." Would Jesus be so presumptuous that He dare ask for something God had expressly forbid?

Turning to Philippians 2:5-11, we see Paul show that it was *this* glory which Jesus laid aside when "he was made flesh" (John 1:14). Because Jesus pre-existed in the essence, the nature, the glory of God, and willingly laid this aside, He took on the form of man to become man's saviour.

Jesus had that glory restored so He now rules over all (Phil. 2:10; Matt. 28:18) and has been given a Name that is far above all other names. God would never share His glory with a "lesser god" creature, something He had made with His own hands. But He did share His glory with Jesus, because He was God in essence.

f. Actually, the Jehovah's Witnesses teach that Jesus was created *twice!* In the booklet *The Word, Who Is He?* page 47, they write: *"At His resurrection* Jesus Christ was God's creation or a creation *by* God. *But* at the very beginning of all creation Jesus was God's creation, a creature produced by God." This second creation is because they rejected Christ's physical resurrection. Something had to be substituted so they invented this re-creation theory. One embarrassing fact emerges as a result of this juggling of truth!

If Jesus was re-created a second time when He rose from the grave a glorified spirit creature, then the Jesus who was "made flesh" must still be nonexistent in the grace. (The Society teaches His body might have been dissolved into gases.) Who is this Jesus that is now? Is He the Jesus that originally was, but became nonexistent when Jesus was created in the womb of the virgin? Truly this is "another gospel, another spirit, and another Jesus" (2 Cor. 11:4).

2. If Jesus was created there are two absurdities that must

be faced:

a. In Proverbs 8:22 Jesus is called Wisdom, which according to the Jehovah's Witnesses, was created. There was a time, then, when God was without wisdom!

b. In 1 John 1:2 Jesus is called "that eternal life which was with the Father, and was manifested unto us." 1 John 5:20 reads: "This is the true God, and eternal life." That life is IN the Son (5:11), and whosoever has the Son has eternal life (5:12). If there was a time when Jesus was not, then there was a time when Jehovah was without eternal life. But then He couldn't be the "true God and eternal life." How can eternal life have either a beginning or an ending?

3. If Jesus was created then the problem of creature worship must be faced.

a. The word "worship" occurs about 60 times and is used of adoration and respect due only the Creator God. If it can be shown from the Scripture that Jesus *refused all worship* and that men were commanded *not* to worship Him, then there is a good case against His Deity. The opposite, however, proves to be true.

b. Men *did* worship Him as God and He readily received that worship. (1) The leper (Matt. 8:2); (2) the ruler of the Jews (Matt. 9:18); (3) the blind man (John 9:38); (4) the disciples in the boat (Matt. 14:33); (5) the Syro-Phoenician woman (Matt. 15:25); (6) both the Mary's (Matt. 28:9); (7) the 11 disciples (Matt. 28:17).

To argue that this was only relative or secondary worship is begging the question. Even secondary worship is idolatry (Luke 4:8).

c. God commanded: "Let *all* the angels of God worship Him" (Heb. 1:6). The same angels who refused to allow John to worship them (Rev. 19:10), readily worshipped Jesus as Lord. WOULD THE SAME GOD WHO FORBAD MEN TO WORSHIP OTHER CREATED BEINGS VIOLATE HIS OWN RIGHTEOUS LAW AND COMMAND THE ANGELS TO WORSHIP JESUS IF HE WERE BUT ANOTHER ANGEL?

d. *The Jehovah's Witnesses are extremely confused about the worship of Jesus.* In *The Watchtower* (11/15/63) in their worldwide Great Resolution they said, "That the one living and true God . . . whose name is Jehovah . . . Him alone will we worship: for Him only will we be witnesses . . . " Yet the Society charter says that both Jehovah and Jesus are to be worshipped. The book *Make Sure of All Things* says on page 85: "Christ to be worshipped as a glorious spirit." Confusion such as this is to be expected when one invents a religion!

e. The Revelation is filled with the wonder and worship of Jesus. "And every created thing which is in heaven, and on the earth, and under the earth, and on the sea, and all things that are in them, heard I saying, Unto him that sitteth on the throne, *and unto the Lamb,* be the blessing, and the honour, and the glory, and the dominion, for ever and ever." Jesus wasn't worshipping *with* the rest of creation; He sat on the Father's throne and received equal worship, honor, blessing and glory.

f. But the most remarkable and unmistakable example of recorded worship is found in John 20:28. Thomas maintained a personal doubt about the bodily resurrection. When confronted by the Living Christ and invited to put his finger in the nail prints and "stop being unbelieving and become believing," he cried, "My Lord and my God!" Jesus accepted this worship and said to him, "Because you have seen me you have believed. Happy are those who do not see yet believe" (John 20:27-29, NWT).

Surely if Jesus knew He was only a created being, He would have rebuked Thomas for such idolatry. Instead He commends him for his belief, not only in His resurrection but for his correct confession. Jesus knew Who He was and received worship.

g. When Stephen died, he cried out, "Lord Jesus receive my spirit!" This is definitely prayer. Paul, and others, called on the Name of the Lord Jesus and were saved! Prayer is never directed to anyone but God.

4. JESUS WAS NEVER AN ANGEL. Even the Watch Tower supposition that He was Michael is based on the meaning of the name "Prince." But Hebrews 1:5, 6 dispels forever such a thought. When did God ever say to an angel, "Thou art my Son"? But He did say to His son, "Thy throne O God is for ever and ever."

a. In Revelation 22:1 we read: "The throne of God and the Lamb." Notice there aren't two separate thrones but one. *Thronou* is singular and the genitive case, meaning personal possession. There is only one throne, equally possessed by God and the Lamb. "He, Jesus, sat down at the right hand of the Majesty on high" (Heb. 1:3).

b. Normally, the Witnesses will counter by explaining this was secondary or relative worship, but on page 177 of *Make Sure of All Things,* "relative" worship is condemned. On the next page, bowing before men or even angels as "relative" worship is forbidden, yet on page 85 they say Christ is to be worshipped as a glorious spirit.

5. Why did the Jews demand Jesus' death? Because he claimed equality with God! It must be noted that John 5:18 is *not* a Jewish declaration but the Apostle John's explanation. John said Jesus was equal with God.

a. In John 10:30 Jesus said, "I and my Father are one thing" *(The Kingdom Interlinear).* Coupling this with verse 38, " . . . that ye may know, and believe, that the Father is IN me, and I IN Him," establishes the unique oneness Jesus shared with the Father. Remind the confused Witness that unless Jesus reveals the Father He won't and can't be understood (Matt. 11:27). The inserted words "in union with" in the *New World Bible* are not in the Greek text. If the Witness counters by turning to John 17:20-22 and points out that just as Christ and His Body members are one in agreement, purpose, and organization, so Christ and Jehovah are one. If this is true, then why did the Jews react so violently and cry for His death? They could have said also, "We too are in agreement, purpose, and organization with Jehovah." But they understood well enough that Jesus meant equal sharing of Deity.

One of the five laws demanding the death penalty was blasphemy or claiming oneself to be God. Were Jesus merely an angel they would have laughed Him to scorn and that would have been that.

b. The insertion of "a god" in verse 33 of the NWT is typical. Again, had Jesus made Himself "a god" the Jews would have laughed at Him. No human could ever be God but anyone could say they were "a god." The Roman Emperors did! When the Jews asked Him, "If thou be the Christ, tell us plainly," (John 10:24), His answer was, "I and my Father are one thing." *Vincents Word Studies,* Vol. 2, says on page 197 that the unity is of essence, not merely will or power. The neuter "one" is used with a plural verb showing unity of nature, but a difference of Person.

The Greek word for equal is *ison,* meaning "equal in quality as in quantity, to claim for one's self the Nature, rank, authority, which belongs to God" *(Thayer's Lexicon,* p. 307).

If Jesus said what the Witnesses make Him say, the Jews had no ground for demanding His death. However Jesus claimed *ison,* or equality with Jehovah, therefore they argued for His death. If He didn't mean that, why didn't He set the record straight? The Jews cried: "For a good work we stone thee not, but for blasphemy, and because thou, being a man, makest thyself God" (John 10:30-32). Verse 33 clinches the identification: The Father was IN Jesus!

## HIS HUMAN EXISTENCE

1. If Jesus was created then He wouldn't be the first-begotten but the first created. In Colossians 1:15 Paul used *prototokos* (first-born), not *monogenesis* (first created), which he would have used had Jesus been created. Beget is never create! A man begets a man; a cow begets a cow; and God begets God! What God creates isn't God but a creation, therefore *not* a first-born. *Prototokos* may be rendered as "first-

begetter" or "original bringer-forth" so in Colossians 1:15 it is a comparison between Christ and created things. It's preeminence, not creation, that Paul has in mind.

In Hebrew custom the first-born designates dignity, privilege, and lordship. Esau was the first but Jacob was the first-born. Psalm 89:27 positions David as the first-born meaning primacy of position, as does Romans 8:29 where Jesus is the first-born among many brethren.

2. The whole Arian/Watchtower problem stems from a misunderstanding of Psalm 2:7: "Thou art my beloved Son, this day have I begotten thee." If a certain day was *the* day He was created (using Watchtower language) then prior to this day He was nonexistent! Paul clears the air with his statement in Acts 13:33: "God hath fulfilled the same unto us their children, in that he hath raised up Jesus *again,* as it is also written in the second Psalm, Thou art my Son, this day have I begotten thee."

What day does Paul have in mind? The day that Christ's Sonship would be manifested to the world, namely: His resurrection day! Jesus is "declared to be the Son of God with power, according to the spirit of holiness, by the resurrection from the dead" (Rom. 1:4). It was the day of the resurrection – when He was raised AGAIN – to which the second Psalm refers.

a. John 1:1 reads: "Originally the Word was." This doesn't imply that the Word came into being, but that the Word already WAS! Furthermore, the Scriptures are gravely silent about any first-created Son being called the first-begotten. As God (Phil. 2:6), He was "a son given" (Isa. 9:6), the Son of God who "was made flesh and dwelt among us" (John 1:14).

b. 1 Timothy 3:16 declares Who Jesus was: "God manifest in the flesh." The Jehovah's Witnesses argue that this passage should read: "He who was manifest in the flesh" and that is all right. Examining the six predicates in this passage we discover Who was manifest in the flesh. Greek grammar demands agreement between the pronoun and the person spoken of. In verse 15 there are three nouns: "the church," "the living God," and "the truth." One of these is the antecedent to the masculine pronoun "who," and will agree in gender and number.

Church is *ekklesia,* a feminine noun, so this is out. Next is "the living God" which is *Theos,* a masculine noun. The other is *aletheias,* the truth, which is also feminine. Of the three nouns, only *Theos* is masculine. Therefore it was the "living God" Who was manifest in the flesh. The NWT had to add "he who was" to arbitrarily fit in with their "a god" theory. If they allowed "God who was manifest in the flesh" to remain, some Witness might read John 1:14, "and the Word was made flesh and dwelt among us," and discover Who Jesus really is. The evidence is abundantly clear: the pronoun "who" reverts to the antecedent "the living God."

c. Colossians 2:9 has been doctored in the *New World Bible. Theoteuos* always means Deity or State of Godhead so they changed it to *theiotes,* and rendered it as "divine quality." The *New Kingdom Interlinear,* because of scholarship, changed it to "all the fullness of the Godship bodily," which is a little better.

3. Jesus was *not* made the Christ at His baptism as they teach! Even their own NWT refutes their theology. In Luke 2:11 the angels announced Christ's birth to the shepherds with these words: "Because there was born to you today a Saviour, *who is Christ the Lord."* He didn't *become* Christ the Lord: He was born the Christ! At His baptism God announced to the World Who He was!

4. *But doesn't John 14:28 imply inferiority?* "My father is greater than I"? Taken by itself it appears that way, but when seen in the light of other Scripture the mystery vanishes. It is also written, "he shall deliver up the kingdom to God, even the Father . . . then shall the Son also himself be subjected to him . . ."

a. There was a divine order in the Godhead before Christ was made flesh. "The head of man is Christ; and the head of the woman is the man; and the head of Christ is God" (1 Cor.

11:3). Is the woman any less human than the man because she is subordinate to him? Is the woman inferior to the man because divine order has subjected her to her husband? Isn't there equality of being, but a difference of order? Then the question of subordination doesn't touch the question of essential nature. Because Jesus is subordinate to the Father doesn't make Him less than God. In His essence, the Son is equal with the Father, but regarding order in the Godhead He would say, "The Father is greater than I."

b. In Philippians 2:9 the statement, "Wherefore God has highly exalted Him," presents a problem for the Witnesses. "How can Christ be exalted if He were God?" they ask. Paul said He emptied himself. How could one who was "in the form of God" and "was God" and "was with God," empty Himself? Only one way! By becoming a bond-servant, "being made in the likeness of men . . . becoming obedient even unto the death . . . "

He laid aside His equality with God; the glory He shared with God and learned obedience by the things He suffered (Heb. 5:8). What should stagger us isn't the fact of His humiliation but that He died for rebellious men! In this position as a man, He was submitted to the Father. "Lo, I come, to do thy will." Therefore God highly exalted Him when He finished!

5. Jesus said, "Before Abraham was, I AM" (John 8:58), and for this statement the Jews sought to stone Him. They understood the implication – He was God!

In both the NWT and *The Kingdom Interlinear* (footnote page 467), the statement is made that *ego eimi* – "I AM" – is not the same as *ho on* in Exodus 3:14, LXX. This is only partly true! The *ego eimi* of the LXX (the Greek Septuagint translation of the Hebrew) is an exact parallel of Deuteronomy 32:39; Isaiah 41:4; 46:4, where *ego eimi* is the absolute "I AM." The *ho on* (I AM) in Exodus 3:14 means "THE BEING," and how this has any bearing on the NWT translating *ego eimi* as "I have been" is beyond me. The exact parallel is the Hebrew *ani hu*.

The Jews were fully aware of what Jesus was saying. The great "I AM" of Exodus 3:14 and John 8:58 are the same; therefore, they wanted to stone Him.

The impact of His words on them is vividly portrayed in John 18:6. They entered Gethsemane looking for Him. When He said, "I AM," they fell backward to the ground. What frightened them? Only that they knew what He was saying and implying.

6. IF JESUS WAS GOD, WHO RAN THE UNIVERSE WHILE HE WAS DEAD? This question is supposed to be a stumper. Who ran the universe? The same God who ran it before Christ was made flesh! The same God Who was IN Christ (2 Cor. 5:19).

When the Word was made flesh (John 1:14), He took on Himself the form of a slave (Phil. 2:7), the seed of Abraham (Heb. 2:14). Human life clothed His divine life; God was IN Christ! When the man Jesus died, the eternal Spirit continued living; God can't die!

7. Let's take a look at John 1:1. On page 147 of *The Kingdom Interlinear* the Greek reads, "and God was the word." Now note the NWT in the margin, " . . . and the word was *a god,"* with a footnote and lengthy explanation in the appendix. Their aim is to make this passage mean one of quality and contrast when it really means one of fellowship and union.

a. THEY PROVE TOO MUCH. On page 1158 they state: "This is unreasonable (Russell's foundations remain): for how can the Word be with the God and at the same time be the God? . . . is not the same god as the God with whom the Word is said to be? . . . the Word or Logos is not the God or God, but is the Son of God, and hence a god."

There is only one God (Deut. 6:4). Neither did Jehovah create another god before Him nor did He do so after Him (Isa. 43:10). "There is none beside me" (Isa. 45:21), and "I am God, and there is none else" (Isa. 45:22). Yet the Watchtower insists God did create another god in the beginning, even Michael the archangel Who became Jesus. Although the

Scriptures emphatically, dogmatically, state that God didn't create another god, and that there is no other Saviour except Jehovah, they now have two gods. A big one and a little one. Even though they claim to believe in one God, their desperate attempt to discredit Jesus leaves them with two gods.

b. If they insist on inserting the indefinite article "a" in John 1:1, show them similar sentence constructions and insert "a" there also.

(1) John 1:18: "No man hath seen *a* God at any time."

(2) Philippians 2:6 " . . . thought it not robbery to be equal with *a* God."

(3) Philippians 2:11: "And every tongue should confess that Jesus Christ is Lord to the glory of *a* God *a* Father."

(4) Romans 8:8: " . . . cannot please *a* God." See Romans 8:33 also.

c. Both Greek and English grammar forbids using articles in the predicate when the verb is intransitive (linking), therefore it takes a predicate nominative which qualifies the subject. The NWT is both poor Greek and incorrect English.

IF THE WORD WAS GOD, HE COULDN'T BE WITH GOD. This sounds logical, however, two different Persons are mentioned, the Word and God. John isn't saying the Logos and God are the same Person but the same essence and nature.

d. "And the Word was with God" isn't speaking of contrast or proximity, but of a vital union. The Word wasn't near the Father, He was in oneness with Him, in the bosom of the Father (John 1:18). The word *pros* (with) in John 1:1 is also found in 1 John 1:2, where eternal life which was with *(pros)* the Father, was manifested unto us. Was there ever a time when God was without eternal life? Therefore, Jesus didn't come into existence originally *(arche),* He was already there.

8. One last Scripture. Jesus said, "I am the good shepherd." Who is this good shepherd? In John 10:16 Jesus said, "There shall be one fold, *and one shepherd.*" In referring back to the original as the *Interlinear* suggests, we discover

Ezekiel 34:23 and Psalm 23 which states, "I will set up one shepherd over them." Who is He?

Isaiah 40:11 says, "Behold, the Lord God *(Adonai Jehovah)* will come . . . He shall feed His flock like a shepherd." "The Lord Jehovah is my shepherd . . . I will dwell in the house of Jehovah forever" (Ps. 23). Peter calls Christ the Shepherd and Bishop of your souls (1 Pet. 2:21, 25). By cross reference the record clearly states there is only one Shepherd, Jehovah-Jesus.

## THE DEATH OF JESUS CHRIST

1. *Christ did not die primarily to vindicate Jehovah's name;* He came to give His life a ransom for many; to save that which was lost; to wit, that GOD WAS IN CHRIST, reconciling the world unto himself (2 Cor. 5:19).

2. He came to destroy the works of the devil (1 John 3:8). In so doing He was tempted in all points as we are (Heb. 2:18; 4:15); bore our sicknesses (Matt. 8:17); literally became sin for us (2 Cor. 5:21); mastered demons by expelling them (Matt. 12:28); died for the sinner (Heb. 2:14); and by His resurrection proclaimed the eternal defeat of Satan (Col. 2:15; Rev. 1:18). Any lying charges Satan made against the Name of God *were* vindicated, but Christ's purpose in being made flesh was: "There is born to you this day a Saviour, Who is Christ the Lord" (Luke 1:11).

3. As the last Adam (1 Cor. 15:45) he was man's substitute. Having no sins of His own, He became sin for us that we might become the righteousness of God through Him (2 Cor. 5:21).

4. He died an innocent Lamb (Rev. 3:18), removing Adam's curse (Gal. 3:13), that through His victory over sin and death we might be made new creatures, a new creation. He *did not die only* for "all kinds of mankind" but for "whosoever will" (John 3:16).

## THE RESURRECTION OF JESUS

1. Contrary to Watchtower theology the resurrection *was not* a re-creation of a nonexistent Christ who had perished in the grave. They offer no explanation of what happened to the body except that God never said what happened to it. BUT HE DID! He raised it from the dead (Rom. 8:11). Their theory isn't a resurrection at all but a re-creation of the soul. A "new" person created in the exact likeness of the former person, BUT NOT HIM!

Christ's bodily resurrection was the heart of Apostolic preaching and remains the bedrock of Biblical Christianity and salvation (Rom. 10:9-10). NOT ONE OF THE APOSTLES WAS MARTYRED BECAUSE THEY PREACHED A RE-CREATION OF JESUS! Many pagan religions already had something akin to that. Had they preached that Jesus was still physically dead but re-created a glorified spirit they wouldn't have been killed. Perhaps a snicker behind their backs, but never death. Their message was: "This SAME Jesus whom you killed, God has raised up. He lives physically!"

2. In Romans 8:11, Paul equated the resurrection with the quickening of our mortal bodies, proving beyond any doubt he believed in the physical resurrection of our Lord.

3. The SAME body that was buried was the SAME body that was raised (1 Cor. 15:4), glorified, immortal and incorruptible, but nonetheless a body (Greek *soma*) (1 Cor. 15:42-44). IF THE BODY OF JESUS WAS NOT RAISED THEN HE DID NOT GAIN THE VICTORY OVER THE GRAVE AND DEATH (Rev. 1:18).

IF the body of Jesus wasn't raised then the Jonah sign on which Jesus hinged His deity is worthless. Jonah was physically raised from Sheol (Jon. 1:17; 2:2 with John 2:19-21).

4. In countering John 2:21, 22, " . . . but he spake of the temple of his body. When therefore he was risen from the dead, his disciples remembered that he said this unto them," they'll say this was the Church-Body that was raised. Russell

engineered this heresy in order to maintain his "lesser god" theory.

a. Such an idea immediately creates another error, namely, that the *church was a part of Christ's atonement.* This was Russell's ransom heresy. Imagine! Even before the church was brought forth it was already part of the atonement.

b. The mystery of the Body-Church was foreign to the thinking of the disciples; it was Paul's revelation (Col. 1:27). When our Lord ascended they were still looking for a physical kingdom that would overthrow Rome (Acts 1:6). The church, however, didn't come into existence until 47 days after His resurrection at Pentecost. Yet John 2:22 says that WHEN He was resurrected the disciples remembered Him saying He would be physically raised. IT COULD NOT BE THE CHURCH. It was not in existence yet!

5. His post-resurrection appearances were more than mere materializations as they teach. This would be deception! Jesus told His frightened disciples to "handle me, and see, that it is I, myself; for a spirit hath *not* flesh and bone as ye see me have" (Luke 24:39). *If He were only a recreated spirit, He lied to His disciples!* If a spirit creature doesn't have flesh and bones why did Jesus deceive them? To help them believe? He still lied because they then believed an untruth.

The Witness remark that Jesus passed into a room without opening the door is proof that He was only a spirit, only proves that He possessed an incorruptible body. "It is sown a physical (natural) body, but it is raised a spiritual body." *Every* believer will possess the same, identical body at resurrection. A body . . . "fashioned like unto his glorious body" (Phil. 3:20, 21).

6. His bodily resurrection doesn't interfere with the sacrifice of His life on Calvary. The Witnesses teach this would be removing the sacrifice from the altar.

a. "Without the shedding of blood there is no remission" (Heb. 9:22). The blood is the ransom price (Heb. 9:14, 20), because the "life of the flesh is in the blood" (Lev.

17:11). IF HIS BODY was the ransom price their assumption would be true, but it isn't! "He purchased the church with His own blood" (Acts 20:28).

b. Hebrews 9:14, "How much more will the blood of Jesus, who through the eternal spirit offered Himself without blemish to God," establishes that it was the blood that was presented to the Father for redemption. Therefore, raising the body wouldn't interfere with the sacrifice.

c. The sacrifice wasn't a perpetual dying: ". . . nor was it that He should Himself suffer often . . . so Christ, having been offered *once* to bear the sins of many . . . " (Heb. 9:25, 28). Please take time to read Hebrews 2:14-18 and note that since Satan was defeated through His obedience and death, any further suffering was unnecessary. Notice the finality of verse 18: "Now where there is forgiveness of these things, there is no longer any offering for sin."

7. His enemies will see Him, even those who pierced Him (Zech. 13:6; Rev. 1:7). The Society says this will be by the eyes of faith, but how, where and when will the Lord's enemies receive enough faith to see Him? How can they see Him when they aren't looking for Him? "Unto those who look for Him shall He appear a second time without sin unto salvation" (Heb. 9:28).

## THE EVIDENCE IS OVERWHELMING! JESUS ACTUALLY ROSE FROM THE DEAD!

8. What rose? His body? No, that must remain on the altar the Society says. Was it His soul then? No, the soul and the body comprise a living soul. One can't exist without the other. Then it must have been His spirit. No, that's only His breath. What rose then? God re-created from His memory a glorified spirit creature, exactly like the original Jesus, BUT NOT HIM!

By implication the Society teaches three Jesus's. The first one was Michael the archangel, created back in the beginning. When Jesus was born a human, that angel-spirit-creature ceased to exist. He had to! Otherwise Jesus had an immortal spirit living in his flesh. So the original Michael-Jesus ceased to exist. In his place was born the human Jesus who also died and CEASED TO EXIST (the Society definition of death). Resurrecting Jesus' body would be removing the sacrifice from the altar, so God re-created *another Jesus* exactly like the One Who walked the earth Who was exactly like Michael who was with God in the beginning. WE NOW HAVE THREE JESUS'S!

WILL THE REAL JESUS PLEASE STAND!

9. Let's take a brief look at 1 Peter 3:18 which is a favorite Watchtower scripture: " . . . he being put to death in the flesh, but made alive in the spirit." "In the spirit" is interpreted to mean He was re-created a glorified spirit creature but note He was raised BY the spirit, IN the spirit – but not A spirit!

Romans 8:11 clears this mystery for us: " . . . if the same spirit that raised up Jesus from the dead dwell in you, it (the same spirit) shall also quicken your mortal bodies BY his spirit that dwelleth IN you." In substance Peter says the same truth as Paul. Christ was killed but the spirit of God IN Him raised Him from the dead, exactly the same way our mortal bodies will be made alive. We are not made alive IN the spirit but BY the spirit.

All my Witness friends must give a satisfactory answer to the question, "What happened to the body of Jesus?" Any private explanation without any Biblical foundation is entirely unacceptable!

a. 1 Corinthians 15:24 can also be answered in the light of Romans 8:11. The contrast is between Adam's life which continues in the flesh and Christ's life which is imparted IN the spirit. The first Adam fitted us for life on earth while the last Adam fits us with life in God's Presence (1 Cor. 15:45).

b. I'm aware that 1 Corinthians 15:50 says that "flesh and blood cannot inherit the kingdom," and I agree. Paul's whole resurrection argument is for those who say there is no resurrection (v. 12). Flesh and blood, without the new birth, without His indwelling Spirit, can't become a new creation. Therefore a change must take place first. Mortal flesh is changed (the same body but with death removed); corruption puts on incorruption (the wage of sin is death but when sin is gone, so is death). It's true that "flesh and blood" can't enter heaven, but also remember that Jesus said, "A spirit does not have flesh and bone as ye see me have." Our Lord's body wasn't re-created spirit but glorified spirit, soul and body, a whole man!

11. *Christ's materializations weren't because His body was unrecognizable, as some claim.* Mary's failure to recognize him could have been the early morning darkness, her own tears, but more likely her grief upon seeing the angels and the empty tomb. Her remark to the gardener, "Where have you laid him?" reveals she didn't *expect* any resurrection. Because she didn't expect such an event she wasn't looking for Him. Why *should* she recognize Him? But wonder of wonder, after she heard His voice, she believed and recognized Him.

a. The disciples on the Emaus road had a different encounter. "Their eyes were holden that they should not know Him" (Luke 24:16). The verb in verse 16 is in the passive tense which denotes the person is being acted *upon* from an external source. The same verb form is found in verse 31 when their eyes were fully opened. Jesus opened their eyes because He had previously closed them. It wasn't that they didn't recognize Him because He materialized in a different form, but because Jesus purposely prevented them from "knowing Him."

b. The Mark 16:12 account is easily understood when compared with the whole truth in Luke 24:16. Likewise in John 21:1-14, though the fact that the disciples didn't recognize Him until the great catch of fish is clear in the light of verse 8 which states that the disciples were "only about three hundred feet away . . . " (NWT). Little wonder they didn't recognize Him, plus the fact they weren't looking for Him!

It isn't our purpose to belabor the point, but unless the bodily resurrection is believed in the heart and confessed with the mouth there can be no salvation (Rom. 10:9-10).

## THE SECOND PRESENCE

1. Because the abundance of proof authenticates that Christ is alive and seen by men, He will also be seen when He returns the second time. One verse from the *New World Bible* should settle the question. "And when the sign of the Son of man will appear in heaven, and then all the tribes of the earth will beat themselves in lamentation, and *they will see* the Son of man coming on the clouds of heaven with power and great glory." The tribes of earth, unbelievers, without faith and unable to see Him through the eye of faith, will actually see Him coming (Rev. 6:15-17)!

2. The supposition that His Invisible Presence began in 1874 A.D. (Russell's date) or 1914 A.D. (Rutherford's date) is basic Watchtowerism. They preach that Jesus rules in the midst of His enemies awaiting Armageddon, even though Jesus said that He would *not* return until after the tribulation (Matt. 24:29-31).

Russell based his assumption upon the discovery of one word in *The Emphatic Diaglott,* an interlinear by another cultist. Wilson translated *parousia* as "presence" in Matthew 24:3 and from that one word Russell reasoned the "secret chamber" theory.

a. When *parousia* is compared with Mark 13:4 and Luke 21:7, which are parallel passages, an amazing fact comes to light. Does the "composite sign" of Matthew 24 mean that "Jesus is already present" or that he is "about to come"? Let's see.

b. *Parousia* is a substantive derived from the participle of a non-action verb of state. The Greek action verb for "come" or "coming" is *erchomai* as used in Matthew 24:30. It means an actual, physical coming. Since *parousia* is a verb of state, it can't possibly express the actual act of coming.

c. Both Mark and Luke use the incontrovertible Greek word *melle* instead of *parousia.* Just as Mark and Luke used a word to express an act of "being near" *(melle),* Matthew's account must agree in content. *Melle* refers to an event about to take place, therefore, *parousia* could not mean the actual act of coming.

d. There are passages where *parousia* can be translated as PRESENCE, but some contexts prevent using it that way consistently. 1 Corinthians 16:17; 2 Corinthians 7:6; 10:10; 1:26; and 2:12 are passages where *parousia* could never mean an invisible presence.

e. HOW CAN ONE BE PRESENT BEFORE HE COMES?

If the sign is that someone is coming then it can't be the sign that the coming one is already present; neither can the sign mean that the one already present is about to come, yet the Society forces that conclusion on the thinking person. "What shall be the sign of your presence *(parousia)* BEFORE you come *(erchomai)?"* Didn't Jesus say His coming *(erchomai,* the action verb for come) would be sudden and unannounced, immediately *after* the tribulation of those days and THEN the sign of His coming would appear, even as summer follows spring (Matt. 24:29, 30)?

f. Mark 13:4 and Luke 21:7 then give us the true meaning of *parousia* as used in Matthew 24:3. The truth demands this! It isn't possible the disciples would have asked Him about His coming when they knew nothing about it. On the day of His ascension they were still looking for a political kingdom. Why would they ask for a "composite sign" when they weren't ready to accept His death, much less a resurrection and second coming?

3. WHAT ABOUT 2 THESSALONIANS 2:1-4? Had Russell and Rutherford studied *parousia* in this context they could have saved themselves untold embarrassment. Paul wrote that the *parousia* (v. 1) and "gathering together unto him" could *not* take place until AFTER the "man of sin who sits in the temple of God" is revealed first (v. 3, 4).

The Society claims the "little flock of 144,000 Jehovah's True Witnesses" with a heavenly calling constitute the "temple." Jesus came to *that* temple in 1914 they say. In other words, there is only one true temple, the true Witnesses constituting the Body of Christ. Keep in mind the main body of Witnesses today are not this company; they are Jonadabs. If they insist on such an interpretation, who was this "man of sin" sitting in the "temple" BEFORE the *parousia* Paul spoke of? At the time of the Watchtower *parousia* in 1914-1918 there were only two men sitting in the "temple of God." Either Russell who died in 1916 or Rutherford who took his place. One of them had to be the "man of sin" who was to be exposed BEFORE the *parousia.*

I realize this is a play on words but it's the only logical conclusion one can accept if a consistent pattern of understanding is derived from their teaching. Either that or there are two temples, both called the temple of God.

The truth is there *will* be a worldwide "man of sin" called the antichrist, not a clergy class but an individual. Whoever he is, he will be completely destroyed by the brightness of Christ's coming (2 Thess. 2:1-8; Isa. 11:4) which will be simultaneous with Armageddon (Rev. 19:20; Dan. 7:11; 8:23-25). When the Watchtower *parousia* took place nothing happened to anyone, much less the antichrist clergy class.

a. The eighth world power, according to the Society, is the United Nations, raised up out of the mortally wounded League of Nations. The Roman Catholic hierarchy, along with organized religion and the World Council of Churches, is Mystery Babylon and the harlot riding on that beast who in the U.N. Scripture declares this "man of sin" and the "beast power" will both be destroyed at the *parousia.* But the United Nations wasn't even in existence in 1914.

b. This eighth world power will rule for 42 months (Rev. 13:5) or 3½ times (Dan. 7:25), which is exactly 1260 days (Dan. 12:7) when it will come to a full end. Both Russell and Rutherford used these figures to establish their chronology table with seven times being 2520 days or double the 3½ times or 1260 days. They counted a day for a year and, dating from the fall of Jerusalem in 606 B.C., they arrived at the date 1914 A.D.

If these times and dates are literal, the United Nations should have ruled exactly 3½ years or 42 months, dating from the fall of 1914 A.D., but it still exists. If the times are prophetical, as both Russell and Rutherford believed, then the 1260 days become 1260 years, and, dating from 1914 A.D., Armageddon will take place in 3174 A.D. (The latest Watchtower timetable dates the war of Armageddon in 1975.) What does all this prove?

Simply that Jesus did NOT return invisibly, secretly and inaudibly in either 1874 or 1914 as the Watchtower prophets predicted. IF 1915 A.D. marked the beginning of Christ's *parousia,* then Armageddon or the *teleos,* the full end, took place in 1918 A.D.

When Christ DOES return *(erchomai,* Matt. 24:30) the nations of the world will become the nations of God and His Christ! Satan will be immediately bound and the Kingdom ushered in with power and glory. Hallelujah!

## CHAPTER 30 – IS MAN A SOUL?

1. Man was created in God's image and for His purpose. His outer man, the physical body, was *formed* from the previously existing dust of the earth and was therefore mortal. His inner man, the spiritual nature, was *created* in God's image and is, of course, eternal. It can, however, die spiritually, which is separation from fellowship with God. Man's soul is his self-consciousness, and his spirit his God-consciousness; they are NOT the same, although the terms are often used interchangeably.

2. BOTH the beast, created after their kind, and man, created in God's image, are called living souls or creatures (Gen. 1:24-26). A comparison of several verses in Genesis where the words "living soul" are used indicates that God gave life to both man and beast by His direct actions. They are "living creatures." Living soul refers primarily to physical

life, but does this necessarily prove that all there is to man is shared with the animals?

Not at all! In Genesis 2:7 man received something from the hand of God that is missing in the animals! God breathed into man's nostrils the breath of lives (Gen. 2:7; Job 32:8). The fact that man was made in the likeness and image of God shows that he is both distinct as well as different from the animals (Gen. 1:26, 27). Man's being in the image of God makes him self-conscious, a trait which all animals lack.

3. Immortality always refers to the physical body which will be received at a future time when Jesus comes to resurrect and glorify man's body (1 Cor. 15:42, 50). Resurrection concerns the body of man, not his soul. "It (the indwelling spirit of God) will quicken (make alive) your mortal (dying) bodies," writes Paul in Romans 8:11.

Man's outer body, the flesh, is kept alive by food, but his inner man, his spirit, is kept alive by "every word proceeding out of the mouth of God" (Matt. 4:4).

4. Again Paul says the outer man, the earthly tabernacle IN WHICH we live, can be dissolved. Meanwhile, the spirit, the inner man, continues to live on in a heavenly "house" which is from heaven (2 Cor. 5:1-2; 2 Pet. 1:14). What Paul teaches is that our earthly, physical body can die and be dissolved into gases, yet we have an "in-between" house in which "we" live UNTIL the resurrection raises our physical body to immortality!

5. It is possible to kill the body, WHILE NOT KILLING THE SOUL (Matt. 10:28; Luke 12:4-12; 8:55). These are the words of our Lord Himself! If man IS a living soul as the Society claims, how did Jesus make this mistake? How is it possible to kill the body but not the soul AT THE SAME TIME?

6. Man's spirit is *formed* within him by God (Zech. 12:1). Christ lives in our spirit (2 Tim. 4:22), which spirit is the life of the body (Jas. 2:26).

7. A most amazing revelation is seen in 2 Corinthians 12:1-7. Paul knew of a man who went to heaven, whether IN

the body or OUT of the body, he didn't know, BUT HE DID GO TO HEAVEN WHERE HE BOTH HEARD AND SAW THINGS TOO GLORIOUS FOR HIM TO REPEAT! He must have believed the inner man, the spirit, could leave the body and remain conscious or he wouldn't have said so, that is unless the Witnesses know something Paul didn't!

Many scholars believe this man was Paul when he was left for dead at Lystra (Acts 14:19). It makes little difference. What does matter is Paul's experimental statement of fact: a man actually went to heaven, EITHER IN OR OUT OF HIS BODY, both are possible!

## IS THE SPIRIT THE BREATH OF MAN?

1. In most Watchtower discussions the spirit of man is simply ignored. At best it's identified as "the breath of life." But *pneuma* (breath) doesn't always mean just the breath! In Matthew 27:50 we read that Jesus " . . . ceased to breath" (NWT)? If *pneuma* always means breath as the New World Committee insists, then John 4:24 should read, "God is a breath," but not even they dared venture *that* far.

a. Did Jesus just stop breathing? To be sure, *pneuma* can mean breath – but not always! Where the gospel writers leave off, Paul commences. In Hebrews 9:12 he tells us that Christ shed His blood but He didn't lie annihiliated in the grave for three days. Rather, He "through the eternal spirit offered himself without spot to God" (Heb. 9:14), and then "by his own blood he entered into the holy place, having obtained eternal redemption for us" (Heb. 9:12). In other words, when Jesus *gave up* His spirit on the cross, He immediately, through that eternal spirit (not breath) Who indwelt Him (Col. 2:9), entered the heavenlies as our High Priest, thereby fulfilling the duties of the High Priest on atonement day. IF His spirit was *only* His breath, then His breath entered heaven with His blood in order to remove our sins.

b. I agree that *pneuma* is the Greek equivalent of the Hebrew *ruahh.* Keeping this in mind, turn to Job 34:14

which forever settles the question: "Are man's spirit and his breath the same thing?"

Job writes: "If he gather unto himself his spirit AND his breath," showing a difference between the spirit AND breath. As a test, try to intelligently substitute breath for spirit in the following passages: Acts 23:8; 7:59; Romans 2:29; 1 Corinthians 5:5; Galatians 6:18; 1 Corinthians 6:20; Revelation 6:9-11. Only the context can determine whether breath or actual spirit is meant. One thing is certain: God is not a breath but a spirit.

## TWO QUESTIONS FOR THE WITNESSES

1. If there is no spirit or soul within man, what leaves the body and is consciously present with the Lord, as Paul states in Philippians 1:23? The NWT rendering of this passage as "releasing," meaning a future time when Paul would be with the Lord is again *their* arbitrary reasoning without the backing of *any* scholar. In fact, 2 Corinthians 5:8 answers the question satisfactorily: "But we are of good cheer, and thinking well, willing to be absent *from* the body and at home with the Lord" *(The Kingdom Interlinear).*

What leaves the body? The inner man, groaning now to be clothed upon with our house from heaven (2 Cor. 5:2). When my inner man is absent from this body-house, then it is present with the Lord. It is folly to say this is the person's life record that goes to be with the Lord. Would Paul groan for his "life record" to be with Jesus? Wasn't it already there recorded in the book (Rev. 20:12)?

2. *Who are the souls that John saw consciously talking, restless, and able to be clothed, in Revelation 6:9-11?*

Their bodies are dead (they cried for vengeance for their blood on the earth, v. 10), yet they are in God's presence. It's interesting to watch the Society conjure up another red herring as they "twist" this truth! "These souls are not ghosts but what John saw was the BLOOD of the faithful Christians who met death for sacrificial purposes." (This reverts back to the heresy that the Church is part of the ransom.)

In referring to Abel's blood crying out there is a vast difference. Abel's blood testified to God against Cain's murder, but it didn't talk, neither was it clothed, neither told to be patient, nor was Abel's blood ever called "a soul." How did this literal blood get into heaven anyway?

The Watchtower fabrication that the robes were the Watchtower resurrection of 1918 is pure fantasy, without either fact or Scripture to authenticate it.

The soul of man is not his blood, nor is the spirit of man his breath! It was not formed from existing materials as was his body; it was placed there by God.

What is man? One created in the image and likeness of God or just a higher form of beast?

## CHAPTER 31 – IS THERE LIFE AFTER DEATH?

1. The idea of soul-sleep began in Eden when Satan deceived the first family by saying, "You will not surely die." Soul-sleep is an unscriptural misunderstanding based on a few Old Testament passages, but Christ brought "life and immortality to light through the gospel" (2 Tim. 1:10). Solomon's musings in Ecclesiastes were those of a doubting intellectual who through human wisdom tried to comprehend spiritual things; the bewilderment of a sensuous man steeped in carnal living (Eccl. 2:1-2).

2. Don't confuse consciousness after death with:

a. IMMORTALITY, which only God has now. We will enjoy it in our now-mortal bodies after the resurrection, or

b. ETERNAL LIFE, which is spiritual, abundant life, belonging only to believers who have been regenerated as a free gift of God, or

c. ETERNAL EXISTENCE, which every man has spiritually in his inner man, and which is not physical or corruptible (1 Pet. 3:4).

3. Enoch was translated that he should not see death (Heb. 11:5). When a Witness points to verse 13, "These all died in

the faith, not having received the promise," he only begs the question. The context speaks of Abraham and his sons not finding their city and has nothing to do with Enoch. Verse 5 says THAT HE SHOULD NOT SEE DEATH!

4. King Saul believed in consciousness after death, otherwise there would have been no purpose in his visiting the witch of Endor to bring up Samuel for guidance (1 Sam. 28:11).

Samuel was dead (v. 15), yet he came up from Paradise (v. 15), spoke to Saul and knew his circumstances (v. 16, 17), and gave him prophetic guidance from the Lord Jehovah (v. 16, 19). No demon would have done that. The witch was frightened, proving this wasn't a satanic impersonation to which she was accustomed, and which the Witnesses believe it was, much less a lying spirit. It was Samuel himself, brought there as an act of Jehovah.

5. Paul said "to be absent from the body is to be present with the Lord" (2 Cor. 5:6-8). If there is nothing to man except the physical body, Paul was mistaken in telling us that one *can* be absent FROM the body and present WITH the Lord.

6. In Philippians 1:21-23 Paul wrote: "to die is gain . . . having a desire to depart, and to be with Christ; which is far better." The NWT implication that Paul was anxious to be released at Christ's coming is confusion as well as incorrect translation. How could Paul's dying be gain, when he would lie unconscious in the grave until the resurrection?

2 Timothy 4:6 establishes Paul's context showing he meant physical death, then " . . . and the due time for my releasing is imminent." Paul had finished his course with honor and was ready to be with Christ.

7. Josephus (37-95 A.D.), Jewish historian, wrote that the Sadducees, a religious sect with whom Jesus dealt, believed "that souls die like the bodies" (*Antiquities,* Bk. 18, 1:4). "They take away the belief of the immortal existence of the soul" (*War,* Bk. 2, 8:14). In Acts 23:8, Luke wrote that the Sadducees "say there is no resurrection, neither angels, nor

SPIRIT." Jesus answered them by saying, "God IS the God of the living and not the dead," taking His answer from the Pentateuch, the only portion of the Scriptures they accepted. He proved their theories wrong because He knew man continued to exist after the death of the physical body!

8. In Revelation 19:20 and 20:10 the beast and false prophet who were thrown alive into the Lake of Fire at the beginning of the Millennium are still there and conscious 1000 years later when the devil is cast in with them.

9. In answering Ecclesiastes 9:5-6, point out the key words "under the sun." The phrase "the dead know not anything" must be seen in this context. "Neither have they any more a portion *forever* in anything that is done *under the sun,"* is the way Solomon expresses it. Understanding this passage as the Society views it leaves them unable to come back to earth again in the New World Society.

10. "For in death there is no remembrance, in the grave who shall give thanks" (Ps. 6:5) is another passage that is easily understood by reading verses 1-4 in context. David confesses his sinful state. If he were to die in this state of unforgiveness he would be unable to praise God in Sheol. Rather than this passage proving cessation of being at death, it states a simple fact. When a body dies and is buried, how can it praise God any more?

11. Because the dead can't communicate with the living doesn't mean the end. Of the physical, yes, but what of the inner man? In Genesis 35:18 we read, "And it came to pass as her soul was in departing, for she died . . . " and again in 1 Kings 17:22, " . . . and the soul of the dead child came INTO him again, and he revived."

In helping the Witness understand that this was more than just the life that was departing and returning, turn to Job 33:18, 22 and show them the distinction between the soul AND the life. If death occurs when a person stops breathing and their blood ceases to flow in their veins, then what leaves or returns? Man doesn't HAVE a soul according to the Society, therefore it can't leave or return. Scripture, however, says "AS THE SOUL DEPARTED." When the soul returned the child lived again.

12. In answering Matthew 10:28, "Fear him who has power to destroy BOTH body and soul in Gehenna," the Witness will say the soul is used meaning the future life of the soul. This is impossible in the light of their own theology. ONLY those who are faithful will be resurrected as a soul in the future; then they can die no more! What force would this warning have in this world if it meant destruction in the grave and HOW DID THEY GET INTO THE NEXT WORLD HAVING BEEN UNFAITHFUL? In their words it would read like this: "Fear not them which kill the body, but are not able to kill the *future life as a* soul, but rather fear him which is able to destroy both *future life as a soul* and body in hell." To qualify the word "destroy" turn to the section on Annihiliation.

13. Finally, Jesus spoke with Elijah and Moses on the Mountain of Transfiguration (Luke 9:30; Matt. 17:9). The bearing down on the word "vision" in verse 9, implying that the experience wasn't real but visionary, is arbitrary. The Greek work *orama,* which means "that which is seen, a spectacle" (see Thayer's page 451), is the word for "vision." It could well be translated, "tell the spectacle or tell the events to no one until after my resurrection." This was no simple vision. They actually saw Jesus talking with Moses and Elijah; they heard their voices. Were the angels of Luke 24:23 any less real? The women saw the vision *(orama)* or angels at our Lord's tomb!

## CHAPTER 32 – IS DEATH ANNIHILIATION IN THE GRAVE?

1. Death is simply the separation of the spirit from the body, as borne out by James 2:26. It is the cutting off from God's purposes; a coming short of the glory of God. Death is the wage of sin and there are three kinds of death mentioned

in the Bible.

a. *Physical death* which is the separation of the spirit, the inner man, from the outer man, the body (Jas. 2:26; Eccl. 8:8; 12:7; Luke 23:46).

b. *Spiritual death* which is separation FROM God because of sin. Adam continued to live physically long after he died spiritually and became estranged from God.

c. *Eternal death* which is the second death. It is eternal separation from God in the Lake of Fire because men refused to accept God's free offer of reconciliation through Christ Jesus. No man is lost because of HIS SINS, but because of *sin,* because he believes NOT on the Lord Jesus Christ (Matt. 10:28; Rev. 20:11-15; Rom. 6:23).

2. All men are born alive physically but they are dead spiritually (Eph. 2:1). *All men* die physically, without exception (Heb. 9:27), but if a man is born anew, a second birth, he'll never die (John 5:24), the second death. Unless a man is born again, he'll also die a second time, eternally.

3. The wage of sin is death (Rom. 6:23; Ezek. 18:18-20), "but if the wicked turn from all his sins that he hath committed . . . he SHALL SURELY LIVE, HE SHALL NOT DIE" (Ezek. 18:21). This Ezekiel passage is a favorite with the Witnesses to "prove" the wage of sin is physical death and NOTHING MORE!

If this is true then what does verse 21 mean? "IF THE WICKED TURN FROM HIS SINS, HE SHALL SURELY LIVE, HE SHALL NOT DIE." This is a prime example of taking a verse out of its context.

All men die physically whether saint or sinner. Yet this promise is that the repentant sinner WILL NOT DIE, HE SHALL LIVE. When understood in context it has nothing to do with physical death, but eternal separation from God.

4. If the wage of sin is merely physical death, then every person would be justified before God when he died and could never be brought before the "Great White Throne Judgment" (Rev. 20:11-14). Hebrews 9:27: "It is appointed unto men to die once, but after this the judgment." If death IS the judg-

ment, what is the judgment that comes AFTER death and why?

## CHAPTER 33 – IS HELL THE COMMON GRAVE OF MANKIND?

1. We've already shown that the wage of sin is eternal death and not "gravedom." The entire platform that hell is always the grave because of a mistranslation isn't sound scholarship.

2. *Sheol* (Hebrew) and *Hades* (Greek) do NOT always mean the common grave. Basically they mean the "abode of departed spirits." Only the context can determine its exact meaning. *Queber* (Hebrew) and *Mnemeion* (Greek) also mean grave or tomb. We'll compare *queber* with *Sheol* and determine whether the two words are interchangeable. If Sheol-Hades *always* means the common grave then the two words can be interchanged at will. If not, then Sheol-Hades can have another meaning.

3. *Queber* means the tomb or grave but never hell.

4. *Taphos* and *Mnemeion* mean tomb, grave, etc., but never hell or *Gehenna,* the Greek word Jesus used for hell.

5. *Gehenna* is the final hell, the Lake of Fire. Originally it was the place where Israel, during the time of Isaiah and Jeremiah, forced their children to pass through the fire in pagan religious rites (2 Chron. 28:3; 33:6). Isaiah says the Valley of Hinnom (Gehenna) was kindled with brimstone (30:33). Later, under King Josiah, it became a dump and place of refuse where the last indignation was awarded criminals; their bodies were cast there and burned (Jer. 19:2-11; 2 Kings 23:10). Jesus first used *Gehenna* as the place where the wicked will finally be punished.

6. Sheol-Hades occasionally means the grave, BUT NOT ALWAYS. The words *queber* and *mnemeion* are often used instead.

## COMPARISON BETWEEN QUEBER AND SHEOL-HADES

1. No *sheol* is ever dug, but *queber* is dug six times.

2. Bodies are never put in *sheol* by man, but men put bodies in *queber* 37 times.

3. No person has a *sheol,* but they had a *queber* 37 times.

4. *Sheol* is NEVER on the surface of the earth, but *queber* is on the surface 32 times.

5. *Sheol* is never used in the plural, but *queber* is plural 29 times. *Sheol* is only one place, the place of departed spirits.

6. God alone puts men in *sheol* (Num. 16:30-33; 1 Sam. 2:6).

7. *Sheol* is a place of consciousness (Ezek. 32:21; 27-31), where hell and grave are contrasted (Isa. 14:9-15; Luke 16:19-31).

8. The body is never said to be *sheol,* and the spirit is never said to be in a grave.

9. In the final judgment (Rev. 20:13), death (which is the grave) and hell (Sheol-Hades) will deliver up the dead. This would be impossible if persons were nonexistent in their graves.

10. The grave *(queber* or *menemeion)* is for dead bodies, but hell is prepared for the devil and his angels (Matt. 25:41-46). By this we see that Sheol-Hades and *queber* are not used interchangeably. They are not the same. Therefore *sheol* is not always the grave.

## GEHENNA – GOD'S FEDERAL PRISON

1. *Gehenna* is never translated as grave, nor can it be.

2. It is the federal prison of eternity, while Hades is the county jail reserving the wicked until final judgment.

3. All men die and go to the grave, but only the wicked go to Gehenna. "Verily I say unto you, If a man keep my saying he shall never see death" (John 8:51). Because all men die regardless (Heb. 9:27), this saying refers to spiritual death. It is the New Testament that informs us the wicked dead will be

raised, judged and forever banished into Gehenna (Rev. 20:5; 12-15).

4. If the grave is hell and hell, the grave, then Jesus' warning of the danger of hell is meaningless. Physical death awaits everyone who goes to the grave anyway. To state that He meant they would have no hope of resurrection would "frighten" only the Pharisees. The Sadducees and many pagans didn't believe in the resurrection, so His threat was irrelevant if taken in Watchtower context. He meant exactly what He said, they were in danger of the hell of fire (Matt. 9:44; Dan. 12:2; Mark 3:29; Jude 13).

5. *Gehenna* has various degrees of punishment; there are few and many stripes (Luke 12:47-48; Matt. 11:22-24). If *Gehenna's* punishment is *only* annihiliation in the grave, Jesus' words have no real meaning. How can there be degrees of punishment when one is nonexistent in the grave? Hell is as hateful to Bible believers as it is to those who vainly reject it. In fact, God hated it so much He sent His only begotten Son into the world that through Him men might find reconciliation.

6. Man is an eternal being, created in God's image, and when he dies a lawbreaker, he dies an eternal criminal. Therefore, God prepared *Gehenna* for the devil and all those who follow him. This eternal prison will provide the eternal restraint they need.

7. THE NATURE OF HELL ISN'T PLEASANT. Isaiah 14 describes the death of Nebuchadnezzar and his descent into the hell (v. 3). Those already there received him with mockery that he had fallen as low as they (v. 9-10). Then he speaks of the worm that is spread under thee (v. 11).

a. "Where the worm dieth not" is no sarcastic reference to worms having immortality. This is a Hebraism, an idiom that expressed a state of never dying.

b. Isaiah 66:24 speaks of hell as a place where the fire is not quenched. Jesus used the same descriptive words as well as "outer darkness," "gnashing of teeth," and a place "where it is better never to have been born than be there" (Matt.

8:12; 13:42; 24:51; 25:30; Luke 13:28).

c. It will be the abode of demons (Rev. 9:1-12). The Watchtower charge that Christians teach that Satan and his demons are keeping the fires of hell hot is another of their smoke screens. Demons, who are fallen angels, *are not in hell yet* but reserved in special keeping until they are judged.

10. *Gehenna* is *not* symbolic of the destruction of error or the purifying of faith because no one ever escapes the final hell (Rev. 10:15; Mark 9:43; Matt. 5:22). Whether literal or symbolic, it is illustrative of intense agony, eternal remorse, and undescribable suffering. There just isn't ANY evidence it ever means annihiliation, extinction or nonexistence in the grave.

## ANNIHILIATION – *NONEXISTENCE*

1. The term means "to reduce to absolutely nothing," "to wipe out of existence." It means there could be no resurrection; there would HAVE to be a re-creation, which would no longer BE A resurrection!

2. "Destroy" and "destruction" do not mean annihilation. Try substituting annihilation or "wiping out of existence" in the following passages: Psalm 78:45; Job 19:10; 21:17; Isaiah 34:2; Jeremiah 17:18. Hebrews 2:14 says Jesus destroyed the devil through death, yet we know that Satan is still very much alive and active. Is he nonexistent? "Destroy" means to render powerless, ineffective.

3. "Perish" doesn't mean annihilation. See 2 Peter 3:6; Luke 15:17; Matthew 9:17 and 1 Samuel 27:1.

4. "Consume" doesn't mean annihilation. See Psalm 6:7; 31:10; and Galatians 5:15.

5. Annihilation contradicts Jesus' teaching of degrees and rewards of punishment (Rom. 2:6; Rev. 20:13).

6. Annihilation would be ENDED punishment and not endless punishment.

7. God is too good to send anyone to Gehenna for eternal punishment; THEY GO THERE WILLINGLY (Rom. 5:8).

He provided everything Divine Justice required in order that man might be redeemed. When His offer of pardon is refused, man willingly chooses the only thing that is left, eternal punishment in Gehenna.

## TORMENT

1. It is this aspect of Gehenna and judgment that frightens the average Witness. They harbor a genuine fear of God and His wrath – and they should – until they personally realize that Jesus bore their sins and their judgment has been passed over.

2. Revelation 20:10 reads: "The devil who deceived them was cast into the lake of fire and brimstone, where the beast and the false prophet are, and they will be tormented *(basanisthesontai)* day and night for ever and ever." According to *Thayer's Lexicon,* which is accepted by the Society as authoritative (see NWT, p. 19), *basanizo* means to torment, to be harassed, to torture, to vex with grievous pains (p. 96).

3. In Luke 8:28, demons cry out to Jesus, fearful of *that* torment, " . . . art thou come hither to torment us before the time?" (Matt. 9:29). If these demons were waiting the final judgment when they would be annihilated in the Gehenna-grave of the Witnesses, why would they cry with such fear? And how could He torment them before the time if death is the torment? They knew exactly what lay in store for them and they feared it. Not annihilation but "grievous vexation with pains."

God is not a fiend because of this conscious punishment any more than a civil judge is a fiend for sentencing a man to hard labor for 99 years. Man reaps exactly what he sows (Matt. 12:37; Gal. 6:8).

## CHAPTER 34 – DID JESUS DIE FOR ALL KINDS OF MEN OR ALL MEN?

1. Another erroneous doctrine of Jehovah's Witnesses is their RANSOM, A-CORRESPONDING-PRICE teaching. Jesus gave Himself, they say, a corresponding price ONLY for all kinds of men. If you'll recall our discussion on the resurrection of Jesus, they handle John 2:21-22 by saying Jesus didn't mean His physical body would be raised, but He meant His Body, the Church. When the 144,000 die, their death and sufferings are part of the supreme sacrifice for sin.

a. This peculiar doctrine of the atonement is held ONLY by the Witnesses and modern Russellites, and is easily answered. Of necessity, NO ONE could be a member of the Body of Christ until AFTER He completed redemption. In Hebrews 10:10-18 we discover that we are "sanctified through the offering of the *body* of Christ ONCE FOR ALL." "So Christ was ONCE offered to bear the sins of many" (v. 28). ONLY AFTER Christ was raised from the dead did He present His blood as the sin offering in the heavenlies. Now comes the big question. HOW COULD THE CHURCH-BODY BE A PART OF CHRIST'S SUPREME SACRIFICE BEFORE IT WAS CREATED? And how could the suffering of the saints after Pentecost and onward be a part of *that* Sacrifice when Scripture says HE DIED ONCE FOR ALL?

b. The ONLY way one can be born again or justified is through faith in His finished work on the cross. Only by confessing with our mouths and believing in our hearts that God raised Him from the dead can we be saved (Rom. 10:9-10), and unless one is born again he is *not* part of the church-body. How can the church be part of the ransom?

c. "For there is ONE mediator, Christ Jesus, who gave Himself (without any help from anyone else), a ransom FOR ALL MEN (not all kinds of men) to be testified to in due time" (1 Tim. 2:5, 6). The blood that cleanses flows from Immanuel's veins; never from Adam's veins.

2. In *The Watch Tower* (2/1/54) there is a vain attempt to void Christ's sacrificial work for ALL men by adding to God's word in 1 Tim. 2:6, "who gave himself a corresponding ransom for *all kinds of people.*" Checking in *The Kingdom Interlinear,* it is easy to see there are no corresponding words for "all kinds of people." This is a deliberate Watchtower addition. Christ died for all men!

The ransom was Christ becoming sin for us (2 Cor. 5:21), having been tempted in all points, yet without sin (Heb. 4:15), was made sick (Isa. 53:10), entered Satan's stronghold and defeated him (Matt. 12:28-29), spoiling principalities and powers, triumphing over them (Col. 2:15), and tasting death for all men (Heb. 2:14), thereby destroying all the works of the devil (1 John 3:8), FOR ALL MEN (1 John 2:2).

The Jehovah's Witness argument that the ransom is ONLY for "all kinds of men" is false and unscriptural. Reconciliation is not, as they teach, partly the work of Christ and partly the work of the Church-Body through human effort. It is "not by works of righteousness which we have done, but according to his mercy he saved us" (Titus 3:5).

3. The works-righteousness program instituted by Rutherford is based on one word, *antilutron,* used only once in the Bible in 1 Timothy 2:5, 6. It must be rejected for the following reasons.

a. The word *antilutron* is only used once and doesn't differ greatly from the simple word *lutron.* Rather than meaning "corresponding price" it really means "substitute-ransom." The last Adam, Christ, took the place of the first Adam as his substitute.

b. Christ was more, much more, than just a perfect man equivalent to Adam. The whole section dealing with His Deity proves this point.

## CHAPTER 35 – DOES THE BIBLE LIMIT THOSE GOING TO HEAVEN TO 144,000?

1. The 144,000 are only *one* of several companies of redeemed saints seen in heaven.

2. The 24 elders are seated on thrones before the Throne (Rev. 5:8-10). They were men because *presbuteros* (elder) is never used of angels. Furthermore, their crowns and thrones are the rewards of redeemed men.

3. These elders are *not* the 144,000 of Revelation 7 and 14, even though both groups have harps and sing, which is why the Society equates them *(Then Is Finished the Mystery of God,* p. 32).

a. They are sitting on *their* thrones before Christ's throne. "And they sung as it were a new song before the throne, and before the four beasts, AND THE ELDERS" (Rev. 14:3). How can they be the same group when the 144,000 sing in the presence of the elders and the beasts?

b. Further, there isn't any mention in Scripture of the 144,000 sitting on either their thrones or Christ's throne! However, like the four beasts, and the elders, and the "great crowd," they are "before the throne." In other words, they are all in the same place at the same time.

c. If the number 24 (elders) is a symbolic number, why wouldn't the 144,000 number be symbolic also? We'll discover that these numbers are not literal but representative of large companies of believers.

4. In Revelation 6:9-11 the souls of those who have been slain for their testimony are under the altar and in the presence of the Lamb, Christ Jesus. (IF CHRIST RETURNED IN 1914 A.D. THEN THESE SOULS MUST BE SOMEWHERE ON THE EARTH, waiting for their fellow servants to be killed as they were, otherwise they are in heaven as the Bible shows.) The Witnesses say this refers to the 144,000 company who were waiting for the resurrection to take place in 1918 when they were given white robes.

a. John saw these "souls" as separated *from* their dead

bodies which were still on the earth and heard them crying for vengeance. They were told to wait until their fellow servants were ALSO KILLED AS THEY WERE. Then, together, they would be resurrected.

b. They were seen as being in heaven under the altar. There isn't any way this can be twisted to mean the 144,000 or the 24 elders. Therefore they *must* be another group of "tribulation saints."

5. The two witnesses were taken into heaven bodily (Rev. 11:11-12). Most Jehovah's Witnesses will say these two witnesses, dead and publicly exposed, were the Society during its difficult years of 1918-1922 when its leaders were jailed for un-American activities during World War I. I wonder how the Society was taken bodily into heaven and how the whole world witnessed it?

6. The "tribulation saints," who were beheaded for their witness for Jesus, sit on thrones reigning with Christ for 1000 years (Rev. 20:4). This group *can't* be the 144,000 who were protected and sealed against the tribulation (Rev. 7:1-5) and seen by John IN HEAVEN before Babylon fell (Rev. 14:1, 8).

a. According to the Society, the Tribulation is that period between 1918 and 1975. This group that John saw IN HEAVEN was martyred during that time (according to the Witness calendar) for refusing to worship the Antichrist or receive his mark (Rev. 13:16-18).

b. Antichrist, the Jehovah's Witnesses say, is not a man but the "clergy class." The Bible says he is a man who doesn't regard the God of his fathers, nor the regard of women *or any other god* (Dan. 11:37). The "clergy of Christendom" DO regard the God of their fathers; they DO regard women and they DO regard God. This "man" will rule during the 3½ year tribulation period (not between 1918-1975) during which time the saints whom John saw on the throne reigning with Jesus will be killed. THEY ARE IN HEAVEN AND THEY ARE NOT THE 144,000 CLASS!

7. Enoch is IN HEAVEN (Heb. 11:5). "By faith Enoch

was transferred so as NOT TO SEE DEATH" (NWT). Pointing to verse 13 doesn't solve their problem. Verse 13 refers to Abraham and his sons not receiving the promise of their city. Enoch was transferred. Where? And IF he didn't see death then where is he? He isn't on earth so he must be in heaven.

8. Abraham, Isaac and Jacob WILL BE IN HEAVEN (Heb. 11:13). These verses alone explode the whole Watchtower fabrication. They were pilgrims on the earth, desiring a better, THAT IS AN HEAVENLY, wherefore God is not ashamed to be called their God. FOR HE HAS PREPARED FOR THEM A CITY (Heb. 11:16). Paul said in Hebrews 12:22 the Christian saints were also looking for a HEAVENLY CITY, the new Jerusalem, the same city Abraham sought.

Jesus said the law was preached until John, then the kingdom was preached, AND EVERYONE FORCES INTO IT (Luke 16:16, *New Kingdom Interlinear)*. The incorrect translation of *pas* as "every sort of person" in the NWT is corrected to "everyone" in *The Kingdom Interlinear.* It's important to note that the Lord Jesus said "everyone" may press into the kingdom of God, rather than "every sort of person," which is merely a Watchtower explanation. Furthermore, Jesus said He wouldn't drink wine again until He could drink it anew with Abraham, Isaac and Jacob, AND ALL THE PROPHETS in the kingdom (Luke 13:28). If Jesus meant what He said in John 3:3, 5 these ancient worthies must be born again before they can either *see* or *enter* the kingdom of God. How this fits with the Society's limiting the kingdom of God to Jesus and the 144,000 associate kings is their problem. Jesus said whosoever will may press into it now!

10. The great crowd of Revelation 7:9-17 must be in heaven also. According to Watchtowerism they are the vast numbers of earthbound-Johnny-come-lately's Watchtower-Jonadab witnesses. IF the 24 elders, and IF the four living creatures, and IF the 144,000 are IN HEAVEN, then the great crowd is there also. Why? The key words are "before the throne."

a. Revelation 5:8-10 and 14:3 both show them "before the throne" IN HEAVEN.

b. Watchtowerism explains this as the footstool quoting "heaven is thy throne and earth is thy footstool."

c. In Revelation 19:1 John heard a "great crowd of much people IN HEAVEN," praising God. Are there two great crowds, one IN HEAVEN and one on earth? In verse 4 the 24 elders and the four living creatures joined with them in their worship. IF the elders and the 144,000 are the same group (they are not as we have proven), then this great crowd *has* to be IN HEAVEN! Throughout the Revelation all these groups are seen "before the throne." If being "before the throne" means being on the earth in the footstool position, then the elders, the creatures and the 144,000 along with the great crowd are all ON THE EARTH! There isn't any other way it can be accepted. The truth is the Scriptures show them all IN HEAVEN "before the throne." Unless there are two different thrones and two great crowds – and untold confusion – they must be different groups in the same place – HEAVEN!

NOTE: In Revelation 7:1 the angels are ordered to withhold the tribulation judgments (which the Jehovah's Witnesses say continue between 1918 and 1975) until AFTER the 144,000 *Jews* are sealed. They were *all* sealed at the same time in the same place *before* the judgments began. Why seal them for protection IF most of them are going to be secretly resurrected to heaven? There isn't *any* evidence in this passage – or any other – that implies this means the dead ones were raised while the living ones are caught up at the time of their death, so this explanation doesn't solve the Watchtower confusion.

Recapping this chapter, we see abundant evidence that there are several companies of redeemed people in heaven. One thing is absolutely certain: the great crowd and the 144,000 are in the same place, "before the throne" IN HEAVEN!

## CHAPTER 36 – WHO ARE THE OTHER SHEEP?

1. Since the Society restricts the number who can be born again, spirit baptized, partakers of the Divine nature, and have a heavenly hope, to exactly 144,000, this group called the "other sheep" or "Jonadabs" was invented as non-elect followers. For them salvation is (1) Study; (2) Association with Jehovah's Witnesses and the privilege of being called a Witness; (3) Changing their way of living through self-effort and (4) Preaching the established kingdom message of the Watch Tower. Justification comes to them by their unbreakable steadfastness during the Millennium.

2. The title "other sheep" is taken from John 10:16 but when taken in context is simple to comprehend. Verse 7 says there is only *one* door Who is Jesus; only one sheepfold (v. 1); and only one means of entrance, through Jesus (v. 9); and one fold and one shepherd (v. 16). The Society has *two* sheepfolds, one in heaven; the other the Watch Tower Society which gathers the "other sheep" in. They have *two* doors. The "little flock" must be born again, spirit baptized and partakers of the Divine nature which is Biblically and experimentally correct. The "other sheep" on the other hand don't need to be born again because they gain everlasting life on earth, the second sheepfold. Entrance into *this* sheepfold is through good works performed as faithful duties to the Watch Tower Society. Therefore, Jesus is not *the door* as He said but only *a* door.

a. The key to unraveling their dilemma is in verse 16, "and there shall be one fold, and one shepherd." The little flock were those Jewish believers who had become His disciples, but Jesus looked forward to the time when He would break down the middle wall of partition (Eph. 2:14), thus making both Jew (the little flock) and Gentile (the other sheep) one in Christ (Gal. 3:28).

b. The *one* sheepfold is His Body-Church (Heb. 10:5). When Jesus ascended to heaven, among the gifts *(domata)* He gave to men for the maturing of the Body-Church were *poimenas,* shepherds or pastors who would remain in that Body until He returns. There is only ONE sheepfold, not two, consisting of both Jew and Gentile.

This whole problem stems from Rutherford's division of his followers into classes to cover his 1925 false prophecy that there would then be a resurrection of the Old Testament worthies. When it failed to happen the whole scene was buried with the cry, "Publish, The King and His Kingdom!" and over the following years it has solidified into a doctrine of salvation that is absolutely impossible to substantiate with Scripture.

## CHAPTER 37 – WHAT IS SALVATION?

1. Bible salvation frees the believer from the guilt and effects of sin. It is not a goal to be attained but a promise to be believed. The Witnesses have deleted grace from their thinking and substituted a system of Theocratic requirements in its place. They hope to be saved, *not from sin,* but in Armageddon IF they prove themselves worthy by Theocratic works. Their hope isn't built on the finished work of Jesus but on being in the Organization which is their Ark of Safety.

2. Bible salvation includes (1) Justification from the penalty of sin (Rom. 5:8; John 5:24; Gal. 3:13) which is always past and completed, (2) Sanctification from the *power* of sin (Luke 10:17-20; Rom. 6:14; 2 Tim. 2:21) which is present and continual, and (3) Glorification, or the final deliverance from the *presence* of sin (Heb. 9:28; Rom. 8:23; 1 Cor. 15:51-54).

3. All salvation is based on the finished work of Christ (Acts 4:12; 16:31; 2 Cor. 5:21).

4. It *cannot* be merited, earned, rewarded, deserved, claimed or proven worthy of attaining. It is a free gift received by faith and "not by works of righteousness (right requirements) which we have done, but according to his mercy he saved us, by the washing of regeneration, and re-

newing of the Holy Spirit" (Titus 3:4-5).

The idea that man can prove himself worthy of fellowship with God began in Eden when Adam and Eve sewed fig leaves together in an attempt to cover their nakedness. However God rejected their efforts and personally provided the life of an innocent animal whose skin covered them. In like manner, men today, vainly attempt to appease God with their own righteousness. Man without God continually works to justify his wrong.

5. Salvation *is* a completed work. The Watchtower theory that it is progressive is unscriptural, primarily because they have misapplied sanctification with justification. Their use of Philippians 2:12, "Work out your salvation with fear and trembling," has no reference to justification but daily growth. One can't work out something he doesn't possess. The same is true with Matthew 10:22 and Luke 13:23, "He that endures until the end shall be saved," which refers to the steadfastness of those during the tribulation.

a. The Greek verb tenses prove that justification is a past experience for the true believer. *Esosen* and *sosantos* are both aorist tense signifying a *completed past event.* If salvation was progressive and future the Greek tense would be the middle voice but it isn't.

b. For further proof that justification is apart from our human efforts see Romans 3:28 in the NWT: "For we reckon that a man is declared righteous by faith apart from the works of law." *Dikaioo* means declared righteous, guiltless, justified and acceptable before God.

c. Titus 3:5 should clear the subject once and for all except for the fact that the New World Translation Committee deliberately deleted two important words. The *New Kingdom Interlinear* exposes their vain attempt. The NWT reads in part: " . . . he saved us through the bath that brought us to life . . . " The Greek reads, *loutrou* (bath) *palingenesias* (of regeneration). *This last word is completely left out!* Regeneration *(anakainoseos)* is modified to read "the making of us new by holy spirit." Had they correctly translated anyone could see how a person is saved: "Not by works of righteousness which we have done, but according to his mercy he saved us, BY THE WASHING OF REGENERATION, AND RENEWING OF THE HOLY SPIRIT." There's only ONE way we can be saved: by being regenerated and renewed by the Holy Spirit.

d. John 5:24 announces a completed justification the moment one believes. "He that hears my word, and believes on him that sent me, *has* everlasting life, and shall *not* come into condemnation, but *is passed* from death unto life." To imply that these texts – and many like them – refer to the 144,000 only begs the question. They too are working for their salvation. Meanwhile the Bible says we HAVE EVERLASTING LIFE and SHALL NOT COME into condemnation and HAVE PASSED FROM DEATH UNTO LIFE. That settles it!

e. This salvation is to be worked out (in us), but only after it's received (Phil. 2:12, 13). We are His workmanship CREATED unto good works (Eph. 2:10) but these works are impossible until AFTER we are born again as a new creature (2 Cor. 5:17).

f. There isn't any contradiction between Romans 4:6 and James 2:24. In Romans, Paul says that no man is justified by or because of his works, while James says that "dead faith" isn't real faith at all but mental assent. The faith that saves is the same faith that instructs us in good works (Titus 2:12). We work FROM an accepted salvation and not TOWARDS some future salvation.

6. At Christ's appearing there will be a judgment *(bema)* where and when ALL believers will be judged according to their works (1 Cor. 3:12-15). Some works will be worthless while others endure yet the person will be saved regardless (v. 15). This passage should correlate the Witnesses' concern about works and the free gift of salvation. A gift to be a gift can't be earned or deserved. *Doron* means "outright free gift." How then can a person work to earn a gift? They can't, but they can earn a reward or fair wage. Salvation is a free

gift, plus and minus nothing (Eph. 2:8), while our rewards are the result of the outworking of that salvation. The various companies of believers seen in heaven are the result of this judgment by Christ. Some will inherit many things; some will inherit few things; some will inherit nothing. Study again Jesus' parables of the talents and the pounds.

## CHAPTER 38 – CAN ONLY 144,000 BE BORN AGAIN?

1. Contrary to Watchtower theology, the new birth is NOT a birth-like realization of heavenly hopes, but a definite regeneration, the making of a new creature (2 Cor. 5:17), an adoption into the actual family of God (Rom. 8:14). Because man's inherited nature is continually bent toward evil (Ps. 51:5; Jer. 13:23), it cannot be successfully re-educated or reformed. Man isn't lost because of anything he does; he is born lost, because of what he is! Therefore, the new birth from above is an absolute necessity before *any* person can have fellowship with God.

2. Nowhere in Scripture is there a division among believers: one a born-again company, the other an unregenerate group who earn their salvation by fulfilling right requirements. This error began with Russell and was perfected by Rutherford in 1935 when he closed heaven. Unregenerate mankind would receive a SECOND CHANCE during the Millennium, they said.

a. In John 3:3-7 Jesus made it clear that "unless a man is born again he cannot see – or enter – the kingdom of God. The Society claims the "ancient worthies," including Abraham, Isaac and Jacob, can never be a part of the Kingdom consisting of Jesus and his 144,000 associate kings. Only the 144,000 are born again; therefore only the 144,000 can "see" or "enter" the kingdom. Yet Jesus said in Luke 13:28 that these "ancient worthies" and ALL THE PROPHETS would sit with Him IN the kingdom.

b. If God becomes our heavenly Father through the new

birth, on what grounds do the Jonadabs identify with Him? It's apparent they've attempted to enter by climbing up some other way rather than entering the single door which is Jesus (John 10:1).

3. The promise made by God that He would bless Abraham and through Him all the families of the earth (Gen. 12:1-3) was the "promise of the Spirit through faith" (Gal. 3:14). That promise belongs to every believer who possesses Christ (Gal. 3:26, 29). If *you* belong to Christ, then "you are Abraham's seed, and heirs according to the promise" (Gal. 3:29). IF only 144,000 are born again and spirit baptized (possessors of Abraham's promise), how does this promise apply to "all the families of the earth" except it include the "whosoever will may come"?

There is only ONE way back into fellowship with God – which is what Adam actually lost in Eden – and that is "by the washing of regeneration (the new birth) and the renewing of the Holy Spirit (receiving Abraham's promise or being spirit baptized) (Titus 3:5).

4. Everlasting life, which "is in his son" is the free gift of God to all (1 John 1:3; 5:11; John 3:36). Receiving Him into your life is more than studying ABOUT Him or taking in knowledge ABOUT Him. "He that has the son has life; and he that doesn't have the son of God doesn't have life (1 John 5:12). For example, one may master all there is to learn about George Washington, but unless there is a personal encounter they'll never *know* Washington. That is taking in knowledge WITHOUT KNOWING!

We have the assurance we ARE saved in this life (John 5:24; 11:25; Rom. 8:14-16). It is CHRIST IN YOU THE HOPE OF GLORY (Col. 1:26; Gal. 2:20).

5. HOW IS ONE BORN AGAIN?

a. By receiving Christ's spirit into your being; He is eternal life (John 1:12; 1 John 5:12).

b. Through the Word (1 Pet. 1:23; John 3:3-5).

c. By believing Jesus is the Christ (1 John 5:1; John 20:30-31).

d. By repenting, turning your back on your sins. This is more than just taking in knowledge about right requirements but a conscious restitution (1 John 3:8-9).

e. By confessing both the bodily resurrection and Lordship of Christ over your life (Rom. 10:9-10).

f. Then, and only then, will the Holy Spirit bear witness with your spirit that you are a child of God (Rom. 8:15, 16).

6. This step is most difficult but it wasn't easy for Paul either. As a first century Jehovah's Witness, he too doubted the Deity of Jesus, His bodily resurrection, and salvation by faith in Jesus Christ. He was fully aware of the animosity and vengeance he would suffer at the hands of his friends; but he also knew Jesus was alive! His whole life had been one of keeping right requirements and Jehovah's laws, but suddenly, when he met Jesus on the Damascus Road (Acts 9), he discovered God wanted to save him without his help! All he had to do was make Jesus his supreme Lord – and he did! Unless all Jehovah's Witnesses, like Saul of Tarsus, take the same step of faith and make Jesus their Lord, they'll remain in the ditch of works-righteousness, without eternal life, WHICH IS JESUS CHRIST!

## CHAPTER 39 – HAVE SPIRITUAL GIFTS CEASED?

1. About the only Watchtower doctrine acceptable to some historic Christian churches is their rejection of the charismatic gifts as part of the churches permanent equipment for her ministry and maturity. Their tongue-in-the-cheek explanation is that while God was shifting his favor from natural to spiritual Israel He showered them with gifts. Since the early second century the now-matured church is evidenced by her love and "gift of preaching."

If this private interpretation is challenged to the point of embarrassment, they simply shift their emphasis to the completion of the canon of Scripture. Consequently, any and all gifts of the Spirit today are either fake or "of the devil," they say.

2. The *only* Scripture used to validate their reasoning is 1 Corinthians 13:8-13, and only then by mistranslating the adjective "perfect." Nowhere does God imply the charismatic gifts would cease for *any* of their reasons given.

In verse 10 Paul says, "When that which is perfect is come, that which is in part shall be done away." They force this *perfect* to mean *either* the completed canon or the matured church. If *either* of these explanations is true then Paul must have been discussing *either* of them in context but he isn't!

3. Their problem is a result of misunderstanding the true purpose of the charismata (1 Cor. 12:7-10). Without exception they are always either for Worship, Witness or the Work of the local assembly, edifying either the church or the individual (1 Cor. 14:12, 4).

a. Inasmuch as "tongues" are not spoken *to* men but are directed to God as praise and thanksgiving (1 Cor. 14:2, 16, 17) and edify the individual, prophecy is directed to man and edifies the whole church (14:3, 4) as exhortation, edification or comfort. How can these "in-part" gifts reveal the Scriptures? Even women may prophesy (1 Cor. 11:5) yet no woman gave us any of the New Testament.

b. It is true *all* gifts are given for the maturing of the Body-Church but it is not yet mature! The only thing that happened in the second century was the beginning of 1,000 years of apostasy and unbelief. IF the church matured in the second century where was it until the Reformation? When 1 Corinthians 13:8-10 is seen in the light of Ephesians 4:8-15, one single truth emerges: all gifts continue until the Body grows into a "perfect man, unto the measure of the stature of the fullness of Christ."

c. The phrase "perfect man" gives us the clue. It's the same phrasing Paul uses in 1 Corinthians 13:8-10. The word is *teleion,* a neuter adjective. According to *Thayer's Lexicon,* page 618, it means a full end, maturity, finished, wanting nothing necessary to completeness. When we snatch it out of context we have the two ideas mentioned but when we turn to Paul's other writings we determine his intent and usage. Ephesians 4:13 is an example: "Till we all come in the unity of the faith, and of the knowledge of the Son of God, unto a perfect man, unto the measure of the stature of the fulness of Christ . . . "

d. The five-fold ministry named in verse 11 is for the purpose of training, edifying, and developing the body of believers, FOR THE WORK OF THE MINISTRY – *until* – they all come into a mature *(teleion,* perfect) man, unto the full stature of Christ. The goal then, isn't the completed canon (that idea isn't even implied), much less the matured church as an organization, which is the only way it matured in the second century. It's the individual who matures "in Christ." In this epistle alone Paul uses "in Christ" ten times, "in whom" six times, "in him" three times. His phrase "unto a mature man" is in exact agreement with this theme he uses.

e. As long as one evangelist, one pastor or one teacher, remains on earth, the job of maturing the body is incomplete. All five ministry offices are seen as one ministry and remain until the Body is matured. Paul doesn't segregate the apostles and prophets, leaving the other three. (It's interesting to note that the apostles and prophets listed in verse 11 were *not* given until AFTER Christ ascended (v. 8), automatically excluding the 12 Apostles of the Lamb as the ONLY apostles. Their ministry was to bear witness of the bodily resurrection of Christ while these apostles were foundation builders given to "mature" the Body into the image of Christ.) These apostles, linked by Paul with the charismatic gifts in 1 Corinthians 12:28-30 were to remain UNTIL the church reached the full stature of Christ.

4. The time of "perfection" will be completed when the in-part gifts are swallowed up in the whole, the full end, when He shall come to be glorified IN His saints (2 Thess. 1:10). Then the illustration "as a child" (Eph. 4:14; 1 Cor. 13:11) will be swallowed up in manhood. "Beloved, NOW ARE WE the children *(tekna* – little infant children) of God, and it doth not yet appear what we SHALL be: But we know

that, when he shall appear, we shall be like him; for we shall see him as he is" (1 John 3:2). "For all creation is waiting for the manifestation of the sons *(huios* – grown sons) . . . even we groan within ourselves, waiting for the adoption *(huiotheses* – son placing), to wit, the redemption of the body" (Rom. 8:19, 23).

Paul said we are *now tekna* (little children of God), but will one day reach *huiotheses* (adult son placing, maturity) when our body is redeemed. Any honest Bible student is forced to concede the church as a whole or in part has never reached *that* state of maturity. Therefore, THE GIFTS MUST REMAIN UNTIL THE TELEION IS REACHED AT HIS APPEARING.

5. History does bear record the gifts ceased during the early centuries, BUT NOT BECAUSE THE CHURCH REACHED MATURITY! Rather it entered into a state of political and religious error. Arius, Sabellius, Anathansius, and Oriegen argued their views of the doctrine of Christ. Infant baptism replaced adult believer baptism. The simplicity of true worship was cluttered with the elaborate, sensually imposing ceremonies with all the outward splendor of the heathen temples around them. Ministers became priests, a term never used before 200 A.D. Church buildings were built after Constantine's edict to house the structured, unbending services. For the next four centuries religious politics rocked the church. Faith died! The gifts ceased! The desire for them was gone; neither zealousness nor faith was present (1 Cor. 14:1), and whenever true Bible faith vanishes so does God! Gradually they were replaced with cold, lifeless theology and formalism.

Gradually the Imperial Church emerged, something entirely different from the Church of the Acts. Years later Francis of Assisi visited the Pope, Francis in his rags of poverty, the Pope in vestments of richest splendor. Before the Pope was a pile of gold and silver coin.

"See, Francis," said the Pope, "never again need the church say as Peter had to say, 'Silver and gold have I none.' "

"No, Father," responded Francis, "and neither can the Church say to a lame man as Peter could, 'In the name of Jesus, rise up and walk.' "

## CHAPTER 40 – WHAT ABOUT THE ACCURACY OF THEIR BIBLE?

Especially important are the guidelines the Translation Committee set forth in the Foreword of the original 1950 edition.

a. "We offer *no paraphrase* of the Scripture. Our endeavor all through has been to give as *literal* a translation as possible" (p. 7).

b. To restore the divine name "Jehovah" to the text of the New Testament. "The evidence is, therefore that the *original* text of the Christian Greek Scriptures have been tampered with, the same as the text of the LXX has been." (The LXX is a Greek translation of the Old Testament.) "In place of it they substituted the words *Kyrios* (usually translated 'the Lord') and *theos,* meaning 'God' " (p. 18).

Their "new evidence" is a portion, the second half, of Deuteronomy, which contains the tetragrammaton, the consonants YHWH, that comprise the name for God in the Hebrew text. On the basis of this evidence the Committee said, "It proves the original LXX did contain the divine name wherever it occurred in the Hebrew original."

A paraphrase, according to any standard dictionary, means to "state the meaning of a passage in other words; a restatement of the writer's ideas in different words." It's adding words to express what the paraphraser *thinks* or *assumes* the passage says. To be literal means to be strict, precise, and exacting, taking words in their actual meaning.

In determining the accuracy of the *New World Translation* (NWT) let's see if they followed their guideline principles.

1. RESTORATION OF THE DIVINE NAME WHEREVER

IT OCCURRED IN THE HEBREW ORIGINAL.

Not once does the tetragrammaton appear in any of the thousands of the Greek texts available. The Hebrew sources the NWT lists (19 of them, pp. 30-33), date from 1385 A.D. and they are all, without exception, translations back into the Hebrew from the Greek text, and are of no value at all.

The consonants YHWH have no parallel in the Greek. Therefore, *kurios* (Lord) and *theos* (God) are used both in the LXX and the New Testament. The Committee compared these words with the Hebrew and the LXX and ended up using Jehovah 237 times in the main text and 72 times in the marginal readings. HOWEVER THEY WERE NOT CONSISTENT!

a. In Philippians 2:1, 10 and Romans 14:9-11 are two passages indisputably taken from Isaiah 45:22-25 where the name Jehovah is used. In Romans 14:11 we read: "As I live, says Jehovah, to me every knee will bend down, and every tongue will make open acknowledgment to God."

If *kurios* in verse 11 is properly restored as Jehovah, because the divine name is so stated in Isaiah, *then* verse 9 should have been translated "that he might be Jehovah over both the dead and the living." Why didn't they? Because Paul is speaking of Jesus and this would deny their denial of the Deity of the Lord Jesus Christ.

b. Again in Philippians 2:11 there is the same omission. The Committee, to be consistent as they purpose, should have translated it: "...and every tongue should openly acknowledge that Jesus Christ is Jehovah to the glory of God the Father." It's a direct quote from Isaiah 45:22-25.

In understanding why they would deliberately avoid changing *kurios* to Jehovah as they did in 237 other passages it's necessary to see *The Watchtower,* dated December 1963: "Among the various other ways in which the NWT honors God is by keeping clear from trinitarian bias. *That is why* it renders the controversial phrase of John 1:1, 'The Word was a god . . .' "

If John 1:1 was purposely "juggled" in order to make it

agree with their nontrinitarian teaching of Jesus then the NWT IS NOT A literal translation at all, but filled with paraphrases. In 1950 they claimed integrity, scholarship, and consistency, but 13 years later they publicly admit they changed some passages to avoid the trinitarian truths they contain.

If the Trinity is wrong, why change the Scriptures to prove it? If the NWT is as good as the Committee hailed it, why does the *New Kingdom Interlinear* revert back to the correct Greek translation? Not once does the name Jehovah appear in the Greek text of the *Interlinear.* Why? It wasn't in the original Greek.

c. In Romans 10:13 there is another example. If "everyone who calls on the name of Jehovah will be saved" is the correct reading, then verse 9 should also read: "For if you publicly declare that 'word in your mouth,' that Jesus is Jehovah . . . you will be saved." Not even the NWT dared alter Acts 4:12 where "the only name under heaven that has been given among men by which we must get saved is JESUS CHRIST." Which name will it be, Jehovah or Jesus? Or are they the same?

d. If the postulation of the Committee is concordant then 1 Peter 3:15, based on Isaiah 8:13, should read: "But sanctify the Christ as Jehovah in your hearts." The Committee didn't follow the guidelines set forth. In fact, nearly all the additions, the deletions, paraphrasing, and altering of the Greek text deal with those passages which glorify Christ as God. If the Witnesses, however, would accept their own *New Kingdom Interlinear* exactly as published, and lay aside the *New World Translation* in the margin, they would soon find themselves back in the mainstream of Biblical truth.

2. PARAPHRASING AND ADDING WORDS WHERE THE GREEK TEXT DOESN'T WARRANT.

a. Turn to Colossians 1:16, 17 in the NWT. Four times they've inserted "other" between "all things," making it read "all other things" to avoid any trinitarian bias. In later revisions, probably to cover some of the public rebuke from Greek scholars, they added brackets around the world "other," thus admitting they added it. It does cast a ray of credibility on their honesty, inasmuch as the Committee said it "offered no paraphrase."

Their explanation for adding "other" and using Luke 13:2-4 for authentication is confusing. A parallel passage would be Hebrews 2:10 where the words "all things" are found, but this passage definitely refers to God so it was left. Had they been consistent in their additions they would have added "other" here also.

b. Colossians 1:17 is another paraphrase. "By means of him" translates *en auto,* "in him." There isn't another scholar in the world who would accept the Committee's paraphrasing in this verse. It should read simply, "He is before all things, and all things in him exist, and he is the head of the body. . . . "

Some of these additions used in the original 1950 edition have been altered or dropped altogether, but not until after the intended ideas were firmly established in the minds of the Watchtower Jonadabs.

c. In 1 Peter 4:7 they added "complete" to "the end" giving a note of finality to their teaching that the end took place in 1914 while the "full end" takes place in Armageddon.

d. In Matthew 24:6 and 1 Corinthians 15:24 the addition of "accomplished" has been dropped. Neither of these insertions can be allowed in a literal translation but it did help their doctrines.

e. In John 13:18 they translated the *hina* clause as "the result is" rather than "in order that." Whoever did this passage translated the first aorist passive subjunctive as a present indicative "is fulfilled" rather than "may be fulfilled." In at least four passages in John alone where the Greek is identical, he took the liberty of using four different tenses.

John 13:18: "the scripture *is* fulfilled." Present.

John 17:12: "the scripture *has been* fulfilled." Past.

John 19:24: "the scripture *might be* fulfilled." Aorist passive subjunctive.

John 19:36: "the scripture *to be* fulfilled." Future.

Which one is the literal translation? Can such inconsistent scholarship be trusted? Is the NWT accurate then? Hardly, but let's investigate a little further.

f. They've also deleted their paraphrase "who was the mother of Jesus" in Matthew 1:16. It now reads correctly, "of whom was born Jesus." In verses 20 and 24 the added word "home" is retained, as well as the words "actually" and "his" in verse 22, even though they aren't in the Greek text.

All this may seem unblameable enough, but remember this version was hailed as a literal translation and is used by the Witnesses as a voice of authenticity.

3. THE PRINCIPLE OF LITERALITY is noteworthy, HAD THEY FOLLOWED IT! It would, however, have embarrassed their doctrinal position in several controversial phrases.

a. John 1:1, "and the Word was a god," is perhaps their most famous textual problem. Four pages of appendix explain why, but the real truth wasn't made public for 13 years when *The Watchtower* (12/63) stated: "Among the various other ways in which the NWT honors God is by keeping clear from trinitarian bias. THAT IS WHY IT RENDERS THE CONTROVERSIAL PHRASE JOHN 1:1 'The Word was a god . . .' "

b. The Greek doesn't have an indefinite article. The definite article "the" points out *identity.* Whenever an article does not precede a noun, that noun can either be considered as emphasizing the character, nature, essence or quality of a person or thing, as *theos* (God) does in John 1:1. Of all the scholars in the world I know of none who have translated this verse as they have done. The Greek grammatical construction leaves *no* doubt that "the Word was God" is the *only* possible rendering of the text.

The subject of the sentence is Word *(logos);* the verb, was. Because the noun follows an intransive (linking) verb it refers to the subject of the sentence and would *not* take an object but a predicate nominative. For the Committee to "add" the indefinite article "a" is not only unnecessary but poor Greek and English composition, since *theos* is the predicate nominative of "was" in the third sentence clause and must refer back to the subject, "Word."

Most of their explanatory material centers around whether the *definite* article "the" should be omitted in the predicate, but that isn't the problem. They've inserted an *indefinite* article, therefore the maze of material they present is practically worthless.

*If* the definite article occurred with both Word and God, the implication would be that they are one and the same person, absolutely identical, which is an impossibility. John said that the "Word was with (the) God" (the definite article precedes each noun), and in so affirming he indicates that they are distinct and separate personalities. The Committee attempted to create "another Jesus," giving Biblical authority to their polytheism.

The list of Scripture references where the article "a" was used before the predicate noun is purely arbitrary since none of them have the same sentence construction. The one text they give that is "exactly the same predicate construction" is Acts 28:6, but that too is faulty since the subject is a pronoun and as such has no article.

Some identical examples they could have used are:

John 4:24: "God is spirit," not *a* spirit.

1 John 4:16: "God is love," not *a* love.

1 John 1:5: "God is light," not *a* light.

Matthew 13:39: "The reapers are angels," not *an* angel.

In each example, the noun in the predicate describes some quality or characteristic of the subject. The purpose, then, of the Committee wasn't to establish a literal translation but to establish Jesus as a *lesser god* to "keep clear of trinitarian bias."

If they persist in this type of translation they should be consistent. You can't render *theos* as "a god" in John 1:1 and *theou* as "of God" in Matthew 5:9, Luke 1:35 or John 1:6. *Theou* is the genitive case of the same noun – without an article – and must be translated "of God," and not "of a god" as does the NWT.

c. According to the Society, Jesus is only a re-created, glorified spirit, Michael the archangel, therefore He can't indwell you. Any passage that gives this impression had to be changed.

In John 15:4-5 they rendered *en emoi* "in me" as "in union with me," adding the words "union with." This completely alters the promise of Christ's personal presence with us (Matt. 28:20). The obvious inconsistency can be seen in the *Kingdom Interlinear* in John 17:26 where *en autois* is properly translated as "in them" when it refers to love but immediately afterwards a paraphrase "in union with them" is used when it refers to Christ. Scholars cannot take liberties such as this.

Now look at Romans 8:9 where we read "if God's spirit truly dwells in you" *(en humin).* In verse 10 the *same* two words are paraphrased to read "but if Christ is in union with you." That the Committee knew the difference is evident from their rendering of Galatians 4:19 where *Cristos en humin* is translated "Christ is formed in you." Meanwhile Colossians 1:27 has the identical Greek but they use "Christ in union with you."

Just one or two further examples and we'll be through. In Colossians 2:9 we have an illustration of a *complete word change* to fit their motives. The Greek word *theotetos* is Godship or Godhead but the NWT used "divine quality." *Theotetos,* genitive of *theotes* does NOT mean "divine quality" but actual divinity or deity. Divine quality would be *theiotes* (see Rom. 1:20).

More, much more, could be offered, but this is enough to honestly consider the *New World Translation of the Scriptures* as corrupt, inaccurate, paraphrased and not literal, but a biased travesty of Scripture.

## BIBLIOGRAPHY

The following books and publications were used in the preparation of this text. Most of them are published by the Watch Tower Bible and Tract Society, Brooklyn, New York.

1. *The Kingdom Is at Hand* (1944)
2. *This Means Everlasting Life* (1950)
3. *Let God Be True* (revised edition 1952)
4. *What Has Religion Done for Mankind?* (1951)
5. *Make Sure of All Things* (1953)
6. *New Heavens and a New Earth* (1953)
7. *Jehovah's Witnesses in the Divine Purpose* (1954)
8. *From Paradise Lost to Paradise Restored* (1958)
9. *Babylon the Great Has Fallen* (1963)
10. *Your Will Be Done on Earth* (1958)
11. *Life Everlasting in the Freedom of the Sons of God* (1966)
12. *The Truth That Leads to Eternal Life* (1968)
13. *Then It Is Finished the Mystery of God* (1969)
14. *The Nations Shall Know That I Am Jehovah – How?* (1971)

## BIBLES AND TRANSLATIONS PUBLISHED BY THE W.T.S.

1. *New World Translation of the Christian Greek Scriptures* (1950, revised 1951)
2. *New World Translation of the Holy Scriptures* (1961)
3. *The Emphatic Diaglott* (1942 edition)
4. *The Kingdom Interlinear Translation of the Greek Scriptures* (1969)
5. Assorted *The Watchtower* and *Awake* magazines

## OTHER SOURCES AND MATERIALS USED

1. *Studies in the Scriptures* (now published by the Dawn Bible Students Association, East Rutherford, New Jersey)

2. *The Grace of Jehovah* (Dawn Bible Students)

3. *The Teachings of Jehovah's Witnesses Examined in the Light of the Scriptures* (Raymond Jolly, Laymen's Home Missionary Movement, Philadelphia)

4. *Back to the Bible Way* (Vol. II, 1957-1961, and assorted copies, Roy Goodrich, editor, Fort Lauderdale, Florida)

5. *The Kingdom of the Cults* (Walter Martin, 1966, Zondervan)

6. *Modern Heresies* (John Krumm, Seabury Press, Greenwich, Connecticut 1961)

7. *Other Gospels* (Paul Smith, Marshall, Morgan and Scott, London, 1970)

8. *Thirty Years a Watch Tower Slave* (William Schnell, Baker Book, Grand Rapids, Michigan 1956)

Comments, inquiries or requests for speaking-teaching engagements, books or cassette teaching-tapes should be directed to:

Charles Trombley, Director
Charismatic Teaching Ministries, Inc.
Post Office Box 15308
Tulsa, Oklahoma 74115